Migration, Workers, and Freedoms

The COVID-19 pandemic resulted in a mass exodus of India's migrant workers from the cities back to the villages. This book explores the social conditions and concerns around health, labour, migration, and gender that were thrown up as a result of this forced migration.

The book examines the failings of the public health systems and the state response to address the humanitarian crisis which unfolded in the middle of the pandemic. It highlights how the pandemic-lockdown disproportionately affected marginalised social groups – Dalits and the Adivasi communities, women and Muslim workers. The book reflects on the socio-economic vulnerabilities of migrant workers, their rights to dignity, questions around citizenship, and the need for robust systems of democratic and constitutional accountability. The chapters also critically look at the gendered vulnerabilities of women and non-cis persons in both public and private spaces, the exacerbation of social stratification and prejudices, incidents of intimidation by the administration and the police forces, and proposed labour reforms which might create greater insecurities for migrant workers.

This important and timely book will be of great interest to researchers and students of sociology, public policy, development studies, gender studies, labour and economics, and law.

Asha Hans is Director of the Development Research Institute, Bhubaneswar. She is former Professor of Political Science and Founder-Director of the School of Women's Studies, Utkal University. She is the recipient of the Kathleen Ptolemy Award for refugee studies. Her work is mostly gendered and ranges from refugee studies, migration, climate change, conflict and peace studies, and disability. Her recent books are *The Gender Imperative* with Betty Reardon (Routledge, 2010, 2019), with Kalpana Kannabiran *Social Development Report: Disability Rights Perspectives* (2017), and *Engendering Climate Change: Learnings from South Asia* (co-editor, Routledge, forthcoming).

Kalpana Kannabiran is Professor of Sociology and Regional Director at the Council for Social Development, Hyderabad, a position she has held since 2011. Her work focuses on understanding the social foundations of non-discrimination, structural violence, and questions of constitutionalism and social justice in India. She is the author of *Tools of Justice: Non-Discrimination and the Indian Constitution* (2012) and *Re-Presenting Feminist Methodologies: Interdisciplinary Explorations* (co-editor) (2017).

Manoranjan Mohanty retired as Director of Developing Countries Research Centre and Professor of Political Science at University of Delhi in 2004. A political scientist, China scholar, and a peace and human rights activist, he is editor of *Social Change*, Distinguished Professor at the Council for Social Development, New Delhi, and Chairperson at the Development Research Institute, Bhubaneswar. He is the author of many publications, including *China's Transformation: The Success Story and the Success Trap* (2017) and *Ideology Matters: China from Mao Zedong to Xi Jinping* (2014).

Pushpendra is Professor and Chairperson at the Tata Institute of Social Sciences (TISS), Patna Centre. Earlier he served as Professor at TISS, Mumbai, and Dean of TISS, Tuljapur. He has also been Visiting Fellow at the London School of Economics. His publications include 'Public Report on Basic Education' (1999), *Land Reforms in India, Vol. V* (2001), and *Traversing Bihar: The Politics of Development and Social Justice* (2014). He is co-editor of a series 'Migrations in South Asia' for Routledge. He is also the editor of a bi-annual, peer-reviewed, online journal, *Journal of Migration Affairs*.

Migration, Workers, and Fundamental Freedoms

Pandemic Vulnerabilities and States of Exception in India

**Edited by Asha Hans,
Kalpana Kannabiran,
Manoranjan Mohanty,
and Pushpendra**

Routledge
Taylor & Francis Group

LONDON AND NEW YORK

First published 2021
by Routledge
2 Park Square, Milton Park, Abingdon, Oxon OX14 4RN

and by Routledge
605 Third Avenue, New York, NY 10158

Routledge is an imprint of the Taylor & Francis Group, an informa business

British Library Cataloguing-in-Publication Data
A catalogue record for this book is available from the British Library

Library of Congress Cataloging-in-Publication Data
A catalog record has been requested for this book

ISBN: 978-0-367-64155-9 (hbk)
ISBN: 978-0-367-70288-5 (pbk)
ISBN: 978-1-003-14550-9 (ebk)

Typeset in Times New Roman
by Deanta Global Publishing Services, Chennai, India

Contents

Contributors

Sreekar Aechuri is pursuing studies in law, and is in his 4th year, BABL (Hons.) at NALSAR University of Law. He has an interest in the intersections of law and society and in human rights jurisprudence. He has, since March 2020, been engaged in archiving COVID-19 jurisprudence in courts of different jurisdictions and documenting administrative law on this subject.

Indu Agnihotri taught History at Vivekananda College, University of Delhi, before joining the Centre for Women's Development Studies (CWDS), New Delhi, from where she retired as Director in 2018. Her interests are in history, women's studies, the women's movement, and the study of internal migration from a gender perspective. She was General Secretary of the Indian Association for Women's Studies between 2011 and 2014. She has published works around the themes of the women's movement in India, violence, and gender and migration.

S. Anandhi is with the Madras Institute of Development Studies, Chennai. Her publications pertain to the field of gender studies, with special focus on caste and social movements in colonial and post-colonial Tamil Nadu. She has co-edited three books: *Dalit Women: Vanguard of an Alternative Politics* (2017); *The Strangeness of Tamil Nadu* (2020); and *Rethinking Social Justice* (2020).

Nasreen Chowdhory teaches in the Department of Political Science, University of Delhi. She has a PhD in Political Science from McGill University, Canada. Some of her significant publications include *Refugees, Citizenship and Belonging: A Contested Terrains* (2018) and the edited volume on *Deterritorialised Identities and Transborder Movement in South Asia* with Nasir Uddin (2019). She recently co-edited *Citizenship, Nationalism and Refugeehood of Rohingyas in Southern Asia* (2020).

E. Deepa is a research scholar at the Madras Institute of Development Studies. She has recently been awarded a PhD degree for her thesis on 'Women in the Informal Sector Work: A Case Study of Paid Domestic Workers in Chennai Urban Slum'.

Manish K Jha is Professor and former Dean of School of Social Work, Tata Institute of Social Sciences, Mumbai. His research interests include migration, middle classes in Indian cities, poverty and social justice. He teaches courses on community organisation, social policy, social action, advocacy and movements, and migration and politics. He has extensively contributed in international journals and edited volumes on migration, disaster, community organisation, politics, populism and social justice. His books include *Traversing Bihar: The Politics of Development and Social Justice* (co-editor, 2014).

Praveena Kodoth is Professor at the Centre for Development Studies, Trivandrum. Her research focuses on themes related to gender and development. For nearly a decade now, she has been engaged in policy analysis and field-based research focusing on migrant labour. She recently completed a report on the recruitment and migration of South Indian women domestic workers to the Middle East for the International Labour Organisation which is being published as a Working Paper.

Shamna Thacham Poyil is a PhD candidate in the Department of Political Science at the University of Delhi. Her research focuses on the narrative of statelessness of the Rohingyas and the politics of exclusion in post-colonial Burma. Her publications include 'National Identity and Conceptualization of Nationalism among Rohingya' in *Citizenship, Nationalism and Refugeehood of Rohingyas in Southern Asia* (2020), ed. Nasreen Chowdhory and Biswajit Mohanty, and 'The Global Compact of Refugees: A Viewpoint of Global South', *Refugee Watch* (2020) with Nasreen Chowdhory.

S. Irudaya Rajan is Professor at the Centre for Development Studies, Kerala, India. He has coordinated eight migration surveys in Kerala since 1998, led the migration surveys in Goa, Punjab, and Tamil Nadu, and provided technical support for the Gujarat migration survey. He is editor of the two Routledge series *India Migration Report* (annual) since 2010 and *South Asia Migration Report* (biennial) since 2017. He is one of the expert committee members to advise the Government of Kerala on Covid-19.

Renjini Rajagopalan is an independent policy consultant. She has provided policy research and advocacy support to Indian state governments, international technology companies, UN bodies, and philanthropic organisations like BMGF and MSDF. A recipient of the LAMP Fellowship (2012–2013), she has also been a legislative aide to and led research teams for senior members of the Indian Parliament. She holds a masters in Law from the London School of Economics, majoring in international human rights law.

P. Sivakumar is Head of the Centre for Monitoring, Evaluation and Impact Assessment (CMEIA) and Faculty at the Department of Development Studies, Rajiv Gandhi National Institute of Youth Development (RGNIYD), Sriperumbudur. He was an editorial member of *Migration and Development*, Routledge. His key academic publications include a co-authored book entitled *Non-Resident Tamils and Remittances: Results from Tamil Nadu Migration Survey 2015* (2020) and a co-edited book *Youth Migration in Emerging India: Trends, Challenges, and Opportunities* (2018).

Acknowledgements

This book had its inception in the anguish of migrants during the COVID-19 crisis and the fault-lines in the governance system. The silence of the lockdown and the soft sound of thousands of migrants fleeing from hunger and homelessness compelled us to write and capture the fleeting but dark side of the Indian socio-political economy. This volume is a small tribute to the workers whose lives we have tried to represent. We acknowledge with thanks the contribution of the Development Research Institute, Bhubaneswar, to this collective effort.

We place on record our sincere appreciation of the immeasurable support provided by Shoma Choudhury, Commissioning Manager of Routledge India, at each phase in enabling the publishing of the volume and to Shloka Chauhan of Routledge for her editorial support.

Our contributors have met the purpose of the volume to work with great sensitivity in understanding the issue. We are grateful to them for agreeing to be part of this volume. Keertana K. Tella generously volunteered editorial assistance.

We gratefully acknowledge the financial support received from the Takshila Educational Society, New Delhi which has enabled open access to the online version of the book. We especially thank Shri Sanjiv Kumar, Secretary of the Society for agreeing to our request on very short notice.

1 Introduction

Migration, work, and citizenship: COVID-19 and the faultlines of Indian democracy

Kalpana Kannabiran, Asha Hans,
Manoranjan Mohanty, and Pushpendra

With an exodus of workers never witnessed before in Indian history, COVID-19 has posed deep and grave challenges to our understanding of labour, migration, differentiated citizenship, dignity, security, vulnerability, and deliberative democracy. There are several questions related to basic dignity that arise in this context: Why were workers ousted from cities, throwing them into hunger, starvation, and homelessness at four hours' notice? Nearly half of those in the exodus were women and children. Even while we try to grapple with the human rights implications of those graphic visuals we were witness to for weeks on end, our questions are stacked along two tracks. The first and most obvious one is, of course, health – the range of concerns around the right to health generally, and policies for the containment and treatment of COVID-19-affected persons. The second set of questions pertain to our understanding of the intersections of caste, community, tribe, and class, each intersecting with gender in the reality unfolding before us. At a political moment that sees a stark rise in violence and dispossession against marginalised groups, and a rise in violence against women and non-cis persons, how did the pandemic-lockdown impact concerns of human security informed by gender?

In exploring the unfolding crisis and its long duree impact, we use 'pandemic-lockdown' as a hyphenated descriptor to denote the twin effects of the public health crisis and the forced displacement of the worker population as mutually reinforcing and inseparable from each other in any consideration of state action. In the pandemic, it is health which is fundamental to human experiences. As Sharpe suggests, the health status of populations can serve as an indicator of 'equality, trust and wellbeing' and to improve health 'we need to challenge the underlying injustices and social conditions' (Sharpe 2019: 335). As faultlines in Indian democracy emerged following the lockdown, described by many as brutal, it had all the makings of an unprecedented humanitarian health crisis, with no state response as the preceding two decades of the austerities of the public health system produced an uneven infrastructure in rural and urban India. In its place, the privatisation of healthcare puts access out of reach of the majority, overburdening the already fragile public health system which collapsed without an accessible alternative in place.

The epidemiological approach, in the case of the pandemic, ought to address not only the ending of the coronavirus, but also the violence in domestic and public spaces where the dignity of the displaced worker has been eroded. Mann (1998: 37) argues that violations of dignity should be considered as a form of violence as these infringements 'are pervasive events with potentially severe and sustained negative effects', and future generations may look back at the current limited and narrow understanding of health and wonder how we could have missed seeing violations of dignity as sources of injury to well-being. The violence perpetrated against migrant workers resulted in their stigmatisation as 'carriers of the virus', depriving them of their dignity as human beings and as citizens.

Examining the intersecting vulnerabilities of migrant labour – social location, gender, and place of residence – brings out the nature and magnitude of the faultlines, and the interconnections between layers of urban and rural sectors in the Indian political economy as well as the role played by the Indian state. Firstly, during the COVID-19 pandemic, the health emergency was as challenging as the existential crisis facing labour, especially migrant labour – most evident in the states of Odisha, Jharkhand, Chhattisgarh, Bihar, and Uttar Pradesh, but also at the all-India level. Although estimates vary, from 10 million to over 40 million of inter-state migrants were facing livelihood, displacement, and health crises (Srivastava 2020). Secondly, every agricultural worker, marginal and small farmer, small artisan, and worker in a small enterprise is a potential migrant worker, forced to migrate when the rural economy is unable to ensure their livelihood. It is widely recognised that the crisis had already begun to unfold with globalisation particularly the agrarian crisis before the pandemic. This demographic transition for new livelihoods formed the backdrop of the migrant movement during the pandemic, which threw the migrant labour crisis into sharp focus. The third factor is the invisibilisation of the contribution of migrants workers to urbanscapes.

The abdication of state responsibility is reflected in the manner in which government circulars, such as those for home quarantine, did not take note of people's socio-economic circumstances. Norms of 'social distancing' were insensitive to the fact that migrant workers lived in overcrowded, cramped dwellings, sharing a room or toilet with 10–20 others. Privacy emerged as a major concern with health information being collected on apps without consent. The unregulated use of surveillance tools in the context of health threw democratic norms in peril. Nomani and Parveen (2020), carrying out a critical appraisal of the Indian public health legislation, argue that the constitutional obligation for the enactment of public health and emergency preparedness has not been discharged in the COVID-19 situations.

The pandemic is a moment that is both epidemiological as well as political. Tracking the uneven responses of states globally to the COVID-19 crisis, Ranabir Samaddar suggests that this is in fact an illustration of 'a long-term failure of liberal democracies to sustain public health and life, weakened as they had become due to their commitment to neoliberal agenda and the demotion of public welfare in favour of privatisation,' and more fundamentally points to the incapacity of these regimes to secure life, their task limited to 'arbitrating death' (Samaddar 2020: 5).

Upendra Baxi's reflections on 'exodus constitutionalism' are pertinent. Underscoring the fact that we are speaking of constitutional and core human rights that must recognise the dignity of the human citizen, and that given the unpredictable and as yet unknown effects of COVID-19, all action by the state and judiciary must be tempered by 'epistemic humility' (Baxi 2020). He delineates four attributes of 'exodus constitutionalism' that acquire new meaning during the pandemic-lockdown: first, the reliance of constitutions on the 'constitutional self' and 'constitutional other' – the status of citizenship as set out in Part II of the constitution is a sovereign decision of the state, not a fundamental right. Second, how then do shifts in the construction of citizenship inflect our understanding of the constituents of the exodus? Third, the heightened vulnerabilities of populations affected by the pandemic-lockdown are not adequately captured by terms like 'COVID-19 migrants'. And finally, 'exodus constitutionalism' hinges on the devaluation of citizenship – as we see, for instance, with those forcibly displaced by the pandemic-lockdown. This is the new face of Internally Displaced Persons and must be thought through on those terms (Baxi 2020).

This takes us directly into a consideration of vulnerabilities and social disadvantage. Drawing on nationally representative panel data for 21,799 individuals between May 2018 and April 2020, Ashwini Deshpande and Rajesh Ramachandran find that although the sudden loss of employment hit people across social groups, the vulnerable groups – OBCs, SCs, and STs – suffered significantly more than the upper castes, with the gap between Dalits and upper castes being the highest. They suggest that this may be viewed against the fact of the higher presence of Dalits among the precariat and their overall lower levels of education. The heightening of pre-existing vulnerabilities and inequalities owing to social disadvantages and systemic discrimination against Dalit and Adivasi communities, by their argument, is likely to be exacerbated by the pandemic (Deshpande and Ramachandran

2020). The survey conducted by the Centre for Equity Studies (2020) found that although job loss was pervasive across social locations, the situation of daily wage earners and inter-state migrant workers and Muslim workers was more precarious. Consistent with several other studies conducted across the country, the precarity of labour and insecure conditions of work over a long term made it impossible for workers to withstand the shock of the lockdown – and this was true across rural and urban locales.

While the government announced stimulus packages, questions were raised by development economists such as Jean Dreze (2020) on the basis of their longstanding work on the labouring poor and rights in the informal sector regarding the veracity of these claims.

Gender intersections are critical to an understanding of how the pandemic-lockdown spreads its shroud unevenly across sharply heteronormative spaces – public and private. While it is widely agreed that the informal sector is constituted by the largest section of the Indian workforce that is also predominantly female, the image of the male worker as the norm invisibilises the range of specifically gendered vulnerabilities that confront women and non-cis persons in the informal economy. These could take many forms, from wage discrepancies to specific stigmatising practices to vulnerability to routine sexual violence. Given the disproportionate responsibility of reproductive labour on women (what has rather simplistically been termed the 'double burden' in literature historically), how does this mass displacement affect them disproportionately? What are the specific ways in which the pandemic-lockdown exacerbated insecurity on gender lines? Finally, there is the question of domestic violence. The gendering of pandemic vulnerabilities has been shrouded in the discourse around the 'shadow pandemic'. In a larger context of structural violence and systemic discrimination, the pandemic reinforces stratification, especially in relation to the gendered division of labour – in worksites and within the family. The rise in incidents of domestic violence during the lockdown across the world evoked a comment from Phumzile Mlambo-Ngcuka, Director of UN Women, that there is a shadow pandemic unfolding which locks women and girls into abusive homes (Mlambo-Ngcuka, 2020).

Further, the gendered implications of the pandemic are not restricted to this single issue. Sex work, workplace rights, surveillance, moral policing, extreme vulnerability to sexual violence, and the larger question of 'reproductive justice' come into sharp focus in a pandemic-lockdown situation (Kannabiran 2020).

Violence has been a daily occurrence during the lockdown, heightened by the presence of armed or police forces. Brutality during the lockdown became part of the ethos of a perverse deterrent practised to maintain 'law and order'. The abuse and intimidation targeted groups of people such as migrants, doctors, nurses, frontline workers, and religious communities. Communalisation of COVID-19 has unravelled the injustices and inequities that underpin people's lives. While some states have emphasised the importance of not stigmatising communities on the basis of religion, other states have used this pandemic to aggravate prejudice based on religious identity and vigilantism acting in concert with non-state actors. 'Any attempt to shift accountability of a pandemic of this magnitude to a congregation of persons is deplorable and also counter-productive to public health efforts' (Jan Swasthya Abhiyan and All India Peoples Science Network 2020).

The construction of violence is also by other means such as a language which contributes to a violent situation. Although women frontline workers, nurses, and others involved in taking care of the coronavirus have been designated as 'Corona Warriors', being instrumental in the 'war' against the coronavirus,[1] unfortunately these warriors have been both underpaid and unprotected without the shields necessary when going into so-called 'war zones' created by the virus. It has to be recognised that the use of violent vocabulary militarises the public mindset, and violence becomes the public normal. It is time to recognise that this system of violence will become entrenched, so it must be challenged as the well-being of the human family depends on its removal.

The chapters in this volume attempt to explore fresh contestations around the emerging nature of risk, new terminologies, unimaginable human rights abuses taking place against migrant labour, and the long walk home filled with tragedies. By revisiting work on labour control regimes through the COVID-19 lens, exploring new insights on mobility and new understandings of the migrant body, we hope to initiate a discourse on justice in a larger context of hostile migration environments, exploring constitutional routes, with a focus on vulnerability.

To build on this backdrop, we would need to think through a new method and epistemology that draws attention to democratic and constitutional accountability. It is time to start the pedagogic imagining and structuring of a future world that will open up to new possibilities. The questions before us are: what is normal and just, and how do we protect our fundamental rights when these rights are trampled on? In this context, questions we should be then asking are: what is the appropriate language to create a new alternative? How do we work in collaborative ways? We also need to ask: how do we stop this violence from becoming the 'new normal' in our lives? Are we prepared to re-imagine new worlds where security is dependent not on force but recognition of an interdependent world of collaboration? It is imperative to introduce different methods of development and a new alternative to the 'new normal'. Would this mean creating fundamental changes in our understanding of words such as 'poverty'? This new manifestation is the shift that strikes at the very core of our social structure calling for a reconceptualisation of the vocabulary of change? We recognise that the pandemic has essentially affected our lives and our humanity and is the catalyst we hope for a new equal and just global system.

What lessons can we draw from the migrant workers crisis and through that window about India's political economy? *Manoranjan Mohanty* identifies some specific lessons that cannot be missed by close observers: the paucity of data, the absence of a support system for workers, non-implementation of labour protections, disabling of panchayats – all leading to a cumulative vulnerability of migrant workers. He argues for a new politics of workers challenging the fundamental premises underlying the prevailing political economy that can effectively address the issue of the vulnerabilities that we saw during the pandemic-lockdown.

Nasreen Chowdhory and *Shamna Poyil* focus on the precarity of migrant labour during times of COVID-19 and make a case for 'pandemic citizenship'. To citizen-migrants for whom mobile livelihoods are indispensable to the right to life – Article 21 – Chowdhory and Poyil argue that what appears to be a uniform restriction on mobility is in fact a measure of the disproportionate effect of 'pandemic citizenship' that divests citizen-migrants of any choice and constitutes the use of undue force by the state.

While Part III – the Fundamental Rights chapter – of the Constitution of India is justiciable and strengthens the claim of citizens vis-à-vis the state, *Kalpana Kannabiran* and *Sreekar Aechuri* unravel the faultlines in COVID-19 jurisprudence, by pointing to the uneven application of established constitutional principles across different clusters of cases. What throws the faultlines of constitutional jurisprudence into sharp relief, in their view, is also the hyper-visible class biases in the jurisprudence on the citizens ousted by the pandemic-lockdown.

Indu Agnihotri and *Asha Hans* explore the gendered specificities of the pandemic and the need to rethink questions of 'gendered vulnerabilities' in relation to work, social security, and health. They draw on evidence gathered during the pandemic to examine how the everyday life of migrant women was affected by the lockdown and suggest a new paradigm of analyses from the lens of human security.

Irudaya Rajan, Renjini Rajagopalan, and *P. Sivakumar* foreground the political disenfranchisement of migrants and their invisibilisation by state governments. Examining data of migrant workers, they suggest that portability of political rights and social welfare, although contentious and difficult to implement, might hold the key to the realisation of full citizenship for migrant workers and the elimination of the vulnerabilities they face.

Kerala has been celebrated as inaugurating a new grammar of governance during COVID-19. *Praveena Kodoth* argues that the visibility conferred by the state of Kerala on migrant workers, while it confers a benevolence on inter-state workers, constructs them as 'guests' and 'outsiders'; in a simultaneous move, non-resident Keralites are conferred the privilege of 'belonging'.

S. Anandhi and *E. Deepa* examine the issues faced by domestic workers – a 1.8-million-strong female informal workforce in Tamil Nadu – during the lockdown through a field study in Chennai city. They work as part of a 'dually informalised workforce' in the informal private-domestic sphere with no access to basic labour and social security protections. The chapter attempts to understand how their specific vulnerabilities were exacerbated by the lockdown.

Pushpendra and *Manish K. Jha* explain the journeys taken by migrants as the defining image of pandemic COVID-19. Using the theory of labour control regime they demonstrate how the state adopts the policy of intervention by facilitating as well as restricting journeys of migrants. Drawing from the narratives of workers' struggle for the journey, the chapter explicates the dynamic relationship between state, market, and migrants in times of crisis and emergency due to the pandemic.

Note

1 COVID-19: The New Normal: Militarization and Women's New Agenda in India - Global Campaign for Peace Education (peace-ed-campaign.org) accessed on 29.12.2020.

References

Baxi, Upendra. 2020. 'Exodus Constitutionalism: Mass Migration in Covid Lockdown Times.' *The India Forum.* 03 July. https://www.theindiaforum.in/article/exodus-constitutionalism. Accessed on 14 September 2020.

Centre for Equity Studies. 2020. *Labouring Lives: Hunger Precarity and Despair Amid Lockdown.* New Delhi: CES.

Deshpande, Ashwini and Rajesh Ramachandran, 2020. 'Is Covid-19 "The Great Leveler"? The Critical Role of Social Identity in Lockdown-induced Job Losses.' *GLO Discussion Paper, No. 622.* Essen: Global Labor Organization (GLO). This Version is http://hdl.handle.net/10419/222540. Accessed on 13 September 2020.

Dreze, Jean. 2020. 'Public Services Like Anganwadis Should Not Have Been Shut During Lockdown: Jean Drèze.' *Interview in Scroll.in.* 2 July. Interviewed by Shreehari Paliath. https://scroll.in/article/966207/public-services-like-anganwadis-should-not-have-been-shut-during-lockdown-jean-dreze. Accessed on 13 September 2020.

Jan Swasthya Abhiyan and All India People's Science Network. 2020. 'Proposed Extension of Nationwide Lockdown: Concerns and Demands.' 12 April.

Kannabiran, Kalpana. 2020. 'Reproductive Justice, not Personhood of the Foetus: Lessons Learnt from Safoora Zargar's Experience.' *Livelaw.in.* 27 June. https://www.livelaw.in/columns/reproductive-justice-not-personhood-of-foetus-lessons-learnt-from-safoora-zargars-experience-158991. Accessed on 13 September 2020.

Mann, J.M. 1998. 'Dignity and Health: The UDHR's Revolutionary First Article.' *Health and Human Rights*, 3(2), 3–38.

Mlambo-Ngcuka, Phumzile. 2020. 'Violence against Women and Girls: The Shadow Pandemic: Statement by Executive Director Of UN Women.' 6 April U.N. Women. https://www.unwomen.org/en/news/stories/2020/4/statement-ed-phumzile-violence-against-women-during-pandemic. Accessed on 11 January 2021.

Nomani, Md., Zafar Mahfooz, and Rehana Parveen. 2020. 'Legal Dimensions of Public Health with Special Reference to COVID-19 Pandemic in India.' *Syst Rev Pharm*, 11(7), 131–134. https://www.sysrevpharm.org/fulltext/196-1596599928.pdf. Accessed on 20 Septemeber 2020.

Samaddar, Ranabir. 2020. *Introduction. Borders of an Epidemic.* Kolkata: Calcutta Research Group.

Sharpe, Albie. 2019. 'Public Health and Patriarchy: Militarism and Gender as Determinants of Health Security.' In Reardon, Betty A. and Hans, Asha. *The Gender Imperative: Human Security vs State Security*, 2nd ed. London: Routledge, 335–365.

Srivastava, Ravi. 2020. 'Growing Precarity, Circular Migration and the Lockdown in India.' *The Indian Journal of Labour Economics*. September. Accessed 11 October 2020.

2 Migrant labour on centre stage

But politics fails them

Manoranjan Mohanty

Introduction

In this chapter I discuss the lessons we draw from the experience of the six months of COVID lock-unlock period and then explain them, especially the problematique represented by this scenario by examining the contending perspectives on labour that underlie the prevailing political economy. I argue that it is the politics arising from this perspective that makes it possible for the rulers to keep the workers continuously in a vulnerable condition and suppress their agency. In my view, the alternative is a new politics of labour that fundamentally challenges the political economy of gradation and degradation of labour and economies. It must reject the charity-and-welfare approach of capital and state and affirm the rights approach instead, thus moving from an instrumentalist view to a substantive view of recognising labour as the principal force of civilisational development.

Political organisation is understood here as a form of politics based on a relevant historical and theoretical perspective. No doubt, there are a number of structural factors arising from the political economy which constrain the ability of the migrant workers to overcome the vulnerability that they face. We focus here on the thinking and practice that has evolved over time leading to the present-day condition of the workers.

Vulnerability, agency, and state responsibility

The missing link between vulnerability and agency

The migrant labour crisis in India, triggered by the COVID-19 lockdown in March 2020 was a window that vividly illustrated India's unequal political economy, precarious social ecology, and deepening faultlines (Mohanty, 2020). The principal aspects of that picture became clear in the course of the unfolding scenario of the first six months of the lockdown and unlocking process at which point there was a compelling question as to why such a major social crisis was effectively pushed to the background by the rulers who encountered practically no protest. What was even more striking was the fact that despite the rise in COVID numbers, the regime went ahead with their neoliberal growth agenda of agrarian, industrial, educational, and legal reforms in an accelerated pace while negative economic indicators persisted.

There were signs of workers' agency, especially in the beginning, when most workers chose to leave for their villages when the work units were closed with the announcement of the lockdown. Faced with transportation difficulties and lack of amenities, thousands of migrant workers protested in many parts of the country. But the precarious conditions of their life and work became clear day by day. Their vulnerability enabled the rulers to carry on with their agenda. That between the workers' vulnerability and their potential agency there was a missing link became clearer than before during the pandemic. That is the question I try to explore in this chapter and suggest that a lack of political organisation is the missing link that kept the workers continuously vulnerable and blocked their capacity to play the agency role.

COVID-19 actually put labour on the centre stage of the spectacle of the unfolding scenario in India. In fact, all workers – both in formal and informal sectors of the economy – suffered losses due to the lockdown. Informal sector workers suffered more than the formal sectors workers, and among the former, the migrant workers were the greatest sufferers. After about two months and three spells of lockdown, gradual unlocking began, phase by phase, and the government and industry were keen to reopen the factories, shops, and other enterprises. They needed the workers, especially contract and migrant workers, to return to work. Some even took special steps, such as sending emissaries and making transport arrangement and paying advances, to get migrant workers back so that they could resume their enterprises and construction activities. Thus, the workers were on the centre stage not only as victims of lockdown and the disease but also as essential forces for recovery of the economy and society.

But both the state and the capital tried their best not to acknowledge the centrality of labour even in this situation. The economic recovery package announced by the finance minister in five tranches between 13 and 17 May mostly consisted of incentives to the employers, with a large set of support measures for the big corporations. The few relief measures announced for the migrant workers hardly met their basic requirements. Most conspicuously, exactly at this time came a series of ordinances curbing welfare and organisational rights of the workers. This presented the usual scenario evolved during the neoliberal era, namely incentives for market-driven, capital-led growth with expanding restrictions on labour rights unfolding rapidly during the pandemic. The vulnerability of the workers, informal sector workers in general and migrant workers in particular, was evident at every stage.

Five lessons on migrant labour during COVID-19[1]

Magnitude high, but data missing

Absence of data on migrant labour was a crippling factor during the entire process of the lockdown and reopening. The political system's neglect of collecting data on migrant labour shows how precarious the condition of migrant labour was.[2] There is need for a comprehensive disaggregated data. If the invisibility of migrant labour in India's political economy was not bad enough, the particular way of invisibilisation of women among labour was especially disturbing. It is estimated that 40 per cent of migrant labour were women. But there are no reliable estimates on how many women were independent migrants. It is important that individual and family migration should be separately recorded. Migration of independent women should be specifically compiled.

Denial of right to living wage and dignified livelihood

Violation of the right to life under Article 21 of the Indian Constitution, which includes the right to minimum wages and several other basic conditions identified by the Supreme Court for living with dignity, was evident. There was no heed paid to the ILO norms of decent work. The minimum wage was paid in very few places, such as Kerala. The migrant workers were always forced to work and live under the mercy of the *dalal* or middlemen, officially called labour contractors, who exploited them in multiple ways. The harrowing tales of their life and work came out in vivid details during the lockdown. Payment of minimum wage varied from Rs. 750 in Kerala to as low as Rs. 150 in many places. For the brick kiln workers, the average earning was even less. Women were paid less than men for the same amount of work. In most cases, the dalal paid an advance to the family in the village and escorted the labourer to the destination. The advance amount was paid in the lean season when the poor had no source of income in the village. Thus, the condition of poverty turned the rural poor into bonded labour under the patronage of the middleman to whom the poor household was beholden. This story of 'dadan labour' in Western Odisha has been a longstanding phenomenon which came out in full-blown details during the pandemic.

Absence of a support structure from state, community, or union

The COVID-19 lockdown brought to the open the clear absence of a support structure that could come to the aid of a migrant worker. The worker was at the mercy of the employer, who pleaded inability to pay more than a meagre sum. A string of short-term ad hoc measures was taken by governments and the actual performance depended on the particular civil servant or politician or a voluntary group working in an area. The lesson is that there is a dire need for the state to systematically lay out a support structure for migrant labour in dealing with crises such as the pandemic lockdown. The concept of a community support linkage in the home area, be it the panchayat or the municipal ward that is familiar with the worker and her/his household and can come to their support, does not exist. It was evident when the Odisha government decided to activate the panchayat system to collect information about migrants, organise quarantine centres, and undertake relief measures, giving even the power of the collector in some respects to the sarpanch. By early May the incapacity of the local bodies got exposed. They had become so dependent on the civil servants for implementing welfare programmes that came from above that they did not know how to discharge their new function. Again, Kerala was an exception in this. Where were the trade unions? In India the tragedy for the unorganised sector workers is the absence of effective trade unions. The double tragedy is the governing ideology of the trade unions that do not have any substantial degree of collective welfare programmes for their workers as a part of their normal trade union politics.

Absence of a support structure meant that people placed in unequal conditions got severely unequal support. The upper-caste male got quick relief from their connections while most of the Dalits and the Adivasis and lower OBCs who formed the bulk of the migrant labour were practically left to themselves. Women, especially from SC and ST communities, were left in the most disadvantageous conditions. Muslim minorities in many places had to face difficulties especially because of the Tablighi episode in Delhi in January–February (Rehman, 2020). Muslims returning from Gulf, even if well-to-do in many cases, also faced discriminatory treatment in many states. Most migrants were treated as automatic carriers of the COVID virus and were stigmatised in multiple ways (Srivastava, 2020). Thus, intersecting inequalities on multiple fronts was most conspicuous in case of the migrants.

Poor laws, indifferent institutions: Whose state?

How little support was available from the institutions of state for the migrant workers became clear during the COVID-19 lockdown. Under the Inter-State Migrant Workmen Act of 1979 there were a number of provisions which could provide protection to the workers, e.g., minimum wage, displacement allowance, home journey allowance, suitable accommodation facilities, and medical facilities, among other things. There was also the confusion about the remaking of the labour laws, reducing all the laws into four Labour Codes. Three of them were passed in the Parliament during the boycott by the Opposition parties on 22 September which were welcomed by the employers and condemned by all the trade unions. Firstly, now any enterprise employing less than 300 workers could prohibit organisation of trade unions. Second, the employer's hiring and firing power, especially the power to terminate services, was enhanced. Thirdly, the working hours could be increased from eight to twelve hours and also the working conditions could be altered.[3] This further strengthened the hands of the corporate rich, especially monopolies who had been demanding 'labour reforms' to acquire 'flexibility' in utilisation of labour.

Several such aspects of the political economy came to the open in the COVID moment. This experience alerts the workers organisations, human rights groups, and democratic forces to insist on affirming the basic rights of the migrant workers with strong legal safeguards. In this context the demand for setting up a statutory National Commission of Migrant Labour appears justified.

Unequal political economy, faulty social ecology

The real challenge that came out boldly during the COVID-19 crisis was the need to ensure everyone's right to work with dignity in their home regions. Much of migration is distress migration. Therefore, the prevailing economic process must be re-examined so that people get work in their own village or town or nearby area and do not migrate. Thus, restructuring the political economy to facilitate local employment and local development is the urgent need. Once an area is developed, the migrant labour, more as mobile labour, can go with a higher bargaining power and adequate facilities to help meet the labour demand in certain areas of the country or abroad. We need to initiate restructuring of the rural economy as a whole so as to provide long-term solutions to poverty and unemployment. Rather than aiming at a five trillion GDP, achieving full employment should be our goal (Bhaduri, 2020). MGNREGS can be re-imagined to cover the entire rural economy rather than specific types of jobs listed in a schedule. A diversified rural economy combining traditional and modern technologies can be planned by the panchayats as a zero-unemployment development strategy. The prevailing system of neoliberal, growth-centric economic model steered from above which throws crumbs as relief to the poor under various programmes needs to be transformed into a decentralised self-propelling, sustainable development process at the grass-roots level that makes it possible for people to realise their fundamental rights to live with dignity.

Is the opposition, especially the workers' rights movement, ready to face this challenge? I argue that to acquire that political capacity and enable workers to play the role of agency, there is a need for fundamental questioning of the basic assumptions underlying the current development strategy. Two premises are central to a new politics of workers: It must question the persisting idea of gradation and degradation of labour and economies. Second, it must strongly reject the framework of charity and welfare shown by the employers and the state and insist of the framework of rights to guide transformation of unequal distribution of material, cultural, and political conditions into a more and more equitable and just system. A new politics of labour based on these premises may promise to raise politics of workers from an instrumentalist frame to a substantive frame as a historical agency. COVID-19 may have generated some opportunities to reorient politics of working classes.

Perspective on a new politics of workers

Who are the builders of civilisation – labour or capital? Gradation and degradation of labour and economies in history

There is a continuing struggle about understanding the history of civilisations and their builders. Dominant classes, castes, and races influenced the writing of the history of ideas in such a way that generations were made to believe that the possessors of wealth, knowledge, and status were the builders of civilisations. They set up power systems to enforce these ideas and oppressed large masses of people, terming them as 'physical labourers', 'men of appetite', 'slaves', 'untouchables', 'sudras', 'god's inferior creatures', and so on. The rulers claimed that they had 'wisdom', 'mental faculties', and 'knowledge', and were 'possessors of superior abilities' and 'god's chosen few' to be in the high pedestal and to exercise power. For centuries these ideas flourished in course of the evolution of slave society, caste order, racial order, feudal order, patriarchal order, and many such unequal systems around the world. The distinction between manual labour and mental labour originated from that history. But in all societies such hierarchies had been challenged from time to time. In the fifth century BC, Buddha's frontal attack on the caste order and assertion of equality of all humans was among the first in world history. From then on different justifications of social hierarchy and caste order and their opposition in course of social and religious reform movements in India continued with many reincarnations and gradation of labour got legitimacy.

In post-Renaissance Europe when the 'principle of equality of all men' began to acquire support, it accepted the gradation of labour as a foundational premise. The equality principle was now applicable among one category of people. That premise guided the evolution of capitalism. The distinction between manual and mental labour got many divisions and subdivisions and skills were put in their descending order of value. Mental labour was put far above manual labour, which was degraded. Accordingly, money and status were assigned. Education and training in skills were organised on that basis. Rewards and remunerations were paid according to such gradation. Universities were set up with disciplines in arts and sciences, furthering the hierarchy of labour. Thinkers and theorists were put at a higher pedestal than those who 'applied' that. Colonialism propagated and institutionalised the capitalist notion of gradation of labour throughout the world. This is the brief outline of how the value of labour of vast masses had been suppressed through history.

For three hundred years or so rulers put capital as the central force for building society, making progress and advancing human civilisation. Attempts were made from time to time by social reformers to challenge it and assert that it is labour, human labour, that is the central force driving a society's development. All labour, manual, mental, and spiritual, involved all faculties of the human being. Labour, by definition, is the application of human energy on nature and society, seeking to add value. And that application of energy in every case involves application of the mind irrespective of who performed it. When industrialisation made rapid progress and the size of the working class grew, there was the beginning of some recognition of the contribution of workers to the production process. But the gradation principle still held fast. There were compromise frameworks presented in economic theory that descriptively identified four factors of production: 'land, labour, capital and organisation'. Such a view hides the reality that capital controlled the entire process and how labour, the principal force of production, was suppressed. It believes that capital – the class of entrepreneurs who take initiatives, use capital intelligently, understand the market, take risks, and improve their technology and management systems constantly to generate surplus and make profit – are the builders of the civilisation. The workers are supposed to be with limited understanding of the society and the economy, ill-equipped to take major decisions and fit only to follow production plans and technology developed by the capitalists and their expert advisers.

This history of capitalist treatment of labour had another element built into it, namely divisions among sectors of society and sectors of economy which were also subject to gradation and degradation. Industrialisation in Europe needed labour from the countryside move to cities, which became centres of mass production. Until then, cities were centres of trade and communications located on riverbanks, seaports, and intersections of travel routes. This began the process of urbanisation becoming a mark of progress. Agrarian society was considered backward, and industrial society was a sign of development. Population got gradually concentrated in urban centres. Population migrated to cities and towns to seek jobs and avail better living conditions. Rural-urban contradictions gradually grew in terms of income, access to social services, and standard of living.

This process produced depressed conditions in the rural economy with many traditional occupations disappearing as a consequence of the availability of industrial goods. Colonial regimes enforced this political economy causing de-industrialisation of Asian, African, and Latin American societies. They not only degraded rural agrarian economy as backward but also degraded the local knowledge that guided the multifarious economic and social and cultural processes in the rural and tribal areas as 'unscientific' and 'lagging in the progress of civilisation'. What was remarkable was that the post-colonial era saw the continuation of the same process of industrialisation as development under national leaders. The normal process of expanding employment opportunities attracted rural labour to migrate to the cities and industrial centres. But when rural economy was unable to provide adequate employment, rural labour was forced to migrate in conditions of distress. In regions of continuing poverty distress migration thus became a regular phenomenon. For mining, industries, and construction of roads, bridges, housing and public buildings, and malls and highways more and more labour were needed as the process of development made steady progress.

Gradation of economies continued to grow. Industrialisation in the manufacturing stage was regarded less advanced than in the stage of service industries with finance capital, research and development, education and health services, and especially economic management being an advance over that heralding the Second Industrial Revolution. Manufacturing units which were also polluting industries were shifted to 'less developed economies' in Asia, Africa, and Latin America. Next was the stage of development of information and communication technology, which was described as the Third Industrial Revolution. The current stage is supposedly a further advance with e-governance and artificial intelligence handling 'big data' replacing human labour. This is regarded as the Fourth Industrial Revolution.

COVID-19 gave a rude shock, questioning this eschatology of progress. Many people all over world began to review this notion of development that had not only caused environmental decay, inviting pandemics and climate change, generated multiple inequalities and sources of alienation and violence, but also created many scarcities of essential goods in countries and regions during the health emergency when transport and communications were suspended. It was realised by many all over the world that all the forms of the economies – agriculture, handicrafts, and various forms of industries manufacturing to services, ICT, and AI – were all needed simultaneously and had equal value.

When we put these two dimensions of history together – the gradation of labour and degradation of manual labour, and also gradation of economic activities and degradation of agriculture and rural economy following modern European history – we can understand the predicament faced by migrant labour today.

Instrumentalist view of labour

The dominant belief held by the rulers does not admit the centrality of labour in the production process. Labouring population has to gradually become 'middle class', which the European and US elites believe to be their agenda. This trend was accompanied by strong initiatives by neoliberal regimes for 'labour reforms', which meant giving added power to capital to restrict labour rights.

This perspective on the value of labour in production and the civilisational development has been a core principle of socialist tradition and Marx's critique of capitalism. But when the communist parties translated this principle into policy and practice it turned out to be an instrumentalist view of the role of labour in society. The Party as the vanguard of the working class accumulated power and exercised it in a centralised fashion. Instead of workers at every level exercising self-governance to realise the vision of a socialist society, the Party developed its notion of the 'dictatorship of the proletariat'. The Party leadership set up a centralised state machinery in the name of the workers and developed a planned economy that it claimed had represented the interest of the workers. This system of political economy in the USSR under different leaders over its 70-year history, no doubt had many achievements, but it did not pursue socialist democracy at the grassroots level. Its planned economy had the same economic goals of industrialisation and urbanisation with more and more advanced technology to achieve higher growth as in the capitalist society.

Liberation of labour from multiple bondages of class oppression remained a theoretical objective rather than a lived experience. In China it was called 'socialism with Chinese characteristics' also with a one-Party dictatorship called People's Democratic Dictatorship, pursuing the goals of industrialisation and higher growth. Not only did the extent of social inequality and regional disparity remain high and environmental degradation persist despite many measures to stem it, but the workers did not enjoy many important political rights, including the right to form independent trade unions (Mohanty, 2018). The stated goal of China's 'reforms and open door' strategy was to create an expanding middle class and achieve higher levels of economic growth by using more and more advanced tools of scientific and technological innovation. Thus, the CPC as the vanguard of China's working class is the instrument for building a prosperous industrial society on the model of the Western advanced capitalist society. Deng Xiaoping's theoretical framework that guided this development strategy had identified three instruments of historical development in the modern age: 'science and technology, market and management' that did not have class character according to him.

That thinking enabled China to adopt Western science and technology, management practices, and market techniques from capitalist practice, and make economic progress. The contemporary Chinese political economy is governed not by the labour perspective on development but by the logic of capitalism (Mohanty, 2014). COVID-19 put the Chinese system to test too. The migrant labour who had been stranded in their native places where they had gone for the Spring Festival holidays faced enormous difficulties. Many of them did not return to their workplaces either because they were not welcome back in their former enterprises or because it was too risky under the prevailing health conditions. There were no employment opportunities to absorb them back in their villages and towns either. In fact, the crisis in the countryside during the past two decades had forced a large number of them to migrate to cities seeking work. Thus, China's cities currently have nearly 500 million 'floating population' looking for employment according to unofficial sources, even though the official estimates put them at 250 million (Roberts, 2020).

China presented the paradox of a Communist Party–ruled state where workers both in the city and the countryside faced a great deal of insecurity and tensions. Among them, the women workers, workers belonging to minorities, and workers living in underdeveloped regions suffered even greater hardships, discriminations, and repression in case they resorted to protest action. The Chinese case illustrated not only how gradation of labour continued under what was described as a form of socialism, but even how degradation of manual and similar forms of labour became a part of the education and evolving culture as their education, culture, and media were also patterned after the advanced Western capitalist systems.

Just when this trend of minimising the value of labour was gaining momentum in the neoliberal era of globalisation promoting growth came the COVID-19 pandemic, demonstrating the critical role played by labour in the production process and as a social force. In all countries labour was persuaded to return to work so that the economy could be reopened. It exposed how a well-organised system of exploitation of labour had evolved using the vulnerable sections of society from far off regions of poverty and destitution for accumulation. Using cheap labour to construct modern infrastructure illustrated this phenomenon. Building smart cities out of the labour of the poor and perpetuating unequal living conditions in cities and villages was the norm.

The instrumentalist view of labour is manifest not only in centralised rule in the name of being the vanguard of workers but also in having an undifferentiated and monolithic view of the working class in the name of maintaining solidarity and thus not paying attention to issues of gender, caste, race, religion, disability, sexuality, and other characteristics of labour. In fact, true labour solidarity should result from acknowledgement of the intersectionality embedded in the class struggle against capitalism (Mohanty, 2019).

COVID-19 put to test the entire theory of progress that accompanied capitalism (Patnaik, 2020). The most developed countries suffered the largest fatalities. They regretted that several products that they needed urgently were not manufactured locally. There were reports from many parts of the world on the celebration of indigenous agriculture and tribal people's traditions of production and their knowledge systems as nature friendly and most relevant as a response to COVID-19-type infections. More and more people came to believe that climate change and destruction of natural environment by the current model of industrialisation and urbanisation had created the conditions for the viruses to spread and cause the pandemic (Vohra, 2020). In other words, the gradation of labour and economies was fundamentally challenged.

But the rulers still refused to accept this reality. They were busy trying to recover economic growth and restore 'normalcy'.

Rights vs. charity and welfare

The reopening of the economy would indeed need labour to resume manufacturing and construction and maintain the supply line. For that the prime minister of India announced a few 'welfare measures' (*Kalyan Yojana*) to provide immediate 'relief' to the migrant workers and the poor in general. These included a small, monthly cash payment of Rs. 500.00 into their bank accounts and free ration for 3–6 months. The employment opportunities in the rural areas were supposed to be enhanced to absorb returned workers. At the end of six months since the lockdown was announced, none of these measures proved adequate to meet the requirements of the millions of workers. Behind this way of treating the workers there is a perspective which must be understood. It is about capital and the state providing 'welfare' to the workers rather than respecting their 'rights' as a major contributor to the production process.

History shows how the gradation of labour played out and the value of labour was not acknowledged. As mass production grew and working-class population expanded, factory owners started giving 'welfare benefits' to workers. In feudal systems the estate owners and religious establishments distributed charity among the peasants and workers. After working-class movements were born and launched campaigns for workers' rights, charity was replaced by 'welfare'. Since the successful strike of workers in 1861 in Chicago for the eight-hour working day, this battle between 'welfare' and 'rights' perspectives has gone on.

Foundation of the International Labour Organisation (ILO) in 1919 put the rights perspective on the global agenda of states. But interpretation of its Charter provisions and their implementation have kept the 'welfare' perspective in the governing position, leaving the rights of workers to the specific campaigns in various countries. The Constitution of India puts workers' rights not in the chapter on Fundamental Rights but in Article 41 in the Directive Principles of State policy, which is not justiciable. But as a result of many movements the rights perspective has gained ground. Some important laws have been enacted guaranteeing minimum wages, regulating working conditions, protecting the right to form trade unions, and so on. Some landmark judgements by the Supreme Court such as the *PUDR* case of 1982 guaranteeing minimum wages and the *Bandhua Mukti Morcha* case of 1984 abolishing bonded labour both under Article 21 of the Indian Constitution have further expanded these rights.

Between 2004 and 2009 some major laws were passed to give rights to some basic facilities to citizens of India, such as the Right to Information Act (RTI), Mahatma Gandhi National Rural Employment Guarantee Act (MGNREGA), Forest Rights Act (FRA), Right to Education Act (RTE), and the Food Security Act (FSA). They created a climate of great optimism about the coming of an era of people's rights. No doubt they were very welcome measures that addressed some basic needs of the common people. But very soon it became clear that they did not carry the full support of the capital and the state leadership who thought these were the case of wastage of funds that would violate fiscal discipline and would make the country bankrupt. These 'right-based laws' were partly a product of the political arrangement as that was a time when the Congress-led UPA was also supported by the Left parties. There was also an economic rationality underlying it. The advocates of these laws correctly pointed out that these public investments in human development would build a healthy, educated, and productive workforce for the economy and will also expand the demand side of the economy, giving more purchasing power to the poor and thus pushing the consumption demands especially in the countryside (Bhaduri, 2020; Dubey, 2020). But even in the Congress there was a section which was lukewarm towards this line of thought, especially the MGNREGA. When the NDA regime came to power in 2014, Prime Minister Modi's statement on the MGNREGA in the Lok Sabha made the approach clear. He would continue the scheme, he announced, mainly to remind the country of the failure of the Congress's rule over six decades in eradicating poverty. All those laws faced retreats thereafter. When repealing was opposed by widespread protest, as in the case of the Land Acquisition Law of 2013, it was diluted substantially in practice.

Ironically, during the COVID-19 lockdown, it was the MGNREGA which was of great use when the migrant workers returned to their villages. After reducing the budget allocation for it for many years, the government increased the budgeted allocation by another Rs. 40,000 crores. But that was not enough to absorb the returned workers, many of whom were skilled.

The point of our discussion is that capital and state have not accepted the legitimate demands of workers as 'rights'. Even when laws are passed codifying some rights in them, even when the Constitution is amended to enshrine 'workers participation in management', or some memorable judgements are delivered by the Supreme Court, they are assimilated into the dominant power process. In fact, in 2009 itself it was apprehended by many that these so-called 'right-based laws' may turn out to be mainly the legitimation strategies of the rulers to give further momentum to their neoliberal growth strategy (Gopalan, 2020).

The tragedy is that all the mainstream political parties of India accept the 'welfare' framework for the workers, and they carry on the neoliberal agenda of economic growth propelled by privatisation and globalisation. Unfortunately, this debate between 'welfare' and 'rights' has not occupied series attention of the trade union movement of India. Even when they have struggled for a 'right' of the workers, they have accepted a very limited liberal democratic concept of right as a 'claim recognised by the state through law' rather than viewing rights as 'political affirmations through continuous struggle'. The COVID-19 experience brought out this paradox vividly.

To conclude, the migrant labour crisis vividly brought out how Indian political economy in the era of neoliberal capitalism thrived at the cost of the basic rights of workers. It carefully maintained their vulnerability, effectively suppressing their capacity to play the role of agency. The absence of a politics that fundamentally questioned the perspective of the rulers that graded and degraded labour and economies is what makes it possible for this system to keep going. That perspective based on an intersectional concept of labour needs to affirm rights of labour in a substantive way.

Notes

1 This understanding is not only based on readings on this subject but especially based on the field reports and insights gathered from the weekly web discussions with activists and researchers from various parts of India, including Odisha's KBK region, on the migrant labour situation, organised by the Development Research Institute (DRI) beginning April 2020. Many of the reports are available on www.gabeshanachakra.org. See particularly, Deepak Mishra et al. (2020) and DRI (2020).

2 The Minister of State for labour in a written reply to a question in Parliament on 11 September 2020, on how many migrant workers had died during the lockdown, said that they had no data on migrant labour. For a detailed account see *The Scroll*, 14 September 2020. https://scroll.in/latest/973074/migrant-crisis-no-data-on-deaths-of-workers-during-lockdown-1-04-crore-returned-home-says-centre.

3 In fact, several states, not only BJP-ruled states of UP, MP, Karnataka, and Haryana, but also Rajasthan, Odisha, and Punjab had passed ordinances during the COVID-19 lockdown increasing working hours and relaxing labour laws to improve 'ease of doing business' and fight to pandemic. See http://www.sacw.net/article14312.html.

References

Bhaduri, Amit, 2020. 'The Insecure Worker', *The Indian Express*, 7 July.

Development Research Institute, 2020. 'DRI Statement on the Rights of Migrant Workers in the Pandemic Context and Building a Post-Covid Economy in Odisha, Bhubaneswar'. Retrieved from http://www.gabeshanachakra.org. Accessed on 10 October 2020.

Dubey, Muchkund, 2020. 'Macroeconomic Policies to Reverse the Slowdown of the Indian Economy: Need to Prioritise the Social Sectors'. *Social Change*, 50(2), pp. 300–306.

Gopalan, Aparna, 2020. 'Rights-Politics and the Politics of Rights in Neoliberal India'. *Social Change*, 50(2), pp. 307–321.

Mishra, Deepak et al, 2020. *Surviving the Pandemic: Ground Reports from India's Villages*, Bhubaneswar, Development Research Institute.

Mohanty, Manoranjan, 2014. 'Xi Jinping and the "Chinese Dream"'. *Ideology Matters: China from Mao Zedong to Xi Jinping*, New Delhi, Aakar Books.

Mohanty, Manoranjan, 2018. *China's Transformation: The Success Story and the Success Trap*, New Delhi, SAGE.

Mohanty, Manoranjan, 2019. 'Inequality: A Perspective from the South'. *Oxford Handbook of Global Studies*. New York: Oxford University Press.

Mohanty, Manoranjan, 2020. 'Covid Highlights Faultlines in China, India and the World'. *Social Change*, 50(3), pp. 473–478.

Patnaik, Prabhat, 2020. 'Why Pandemic Crisis Marks a Dead-end for Capitalism'. Retrieved from http://newsclick.in/Prabhat%Patnaik. Accessed on 10 October 2020.

Rehman, Sheikh Mujibur, 2020. Covid-19 has no religion, *The Hindu* (09 July 2020). Retrieved from https://www.thehindu.com/opinion/op-ed/covid-19-has -no-religion/article32024900.ece. Accessed on 28 December 2020.

Roberts, Dexter, 2020. *The Myth of Chinese Capitalism: The Worker, the Factory and the Future of the World*, New York, Macmillan.

Srivastava, Vinay Kumar, 2020. 'Anatomy of Stigma'. *Social Change*, 50(3), pp. 385–398.

Vohra, Chayan, 2020. 'Lessons from a Pandemic: Urgency for Climate Action'. *Down to Earth*, 5 July. Retrieved from https://www.downtoearth.org.in/blog/ climate-change/lessons-from-a-pandemic-urgency-for-climate-action-72149. Accessed on 10 October 2020.

3 Mobile population, 'pandemic citizenship'

Nasreen Chowdhory and
Shamna Thacham Poyil

Introduction

Constituting the lion's share of workforce in India's infrastructure, logistical and supply services, agricultural sector, and even engaging in menial jobs such as that of domestic helps or rickshaw pullers, the unskilled and semi-skilled migrant worker is the most indispensable yet the easily disposable entity in our economic structure. The synergy between 'informality' and 'mobility' has pushed the migrant worker to a vicious cycle of precarious labour, compounded by the 'uncertainty' of one's livelihood, 'insecurity' about one's entitlements and possessions, as well as the 'unsafety' of one's body and health (Bauman, 2000: 161). The usually precarious nature of the work done by migrant labourers elevates to a degree of 'hyper precarity' (Lewis et al., 2015) when subjected to the devastating impact of 'pandemic citizenship'.[1] Drawing on Agamben's construct of exception and constitution of bare life, the chapter conceptualises pandemic *citizens* as those citizens who in the 'state of exception' conjured by the pandemic have forfeited their rights and freedom of movement. The hardships faced by the migrant labour are not just a function of the pandemic but indicative of the compounded structural exclusion that has relegated them to the sociopolitical margins of the state and warranted their categorisation as '*citizen-migrant*'. While the assertion of their agency emerges with their mobility and livelihood paradox, the internal migrants of the country get drawn to the spatial aberration in claiming citizenship rights and entitlements. By subjecting *citizen-migrants* to the vagaries of *pandemic citizenship*, the state dispossesses them of the only modicum of agency that they could exert for the attainment of a dignified life.

Constituting the 'pandemic citizens' from 'citizen-migrants'

In the context of the pandemic, a 'pandemic citizen' has forfeited the indispensability of rights that is central to citizenship. The constitution of pandemic citizenship can be tethered to Foucault's (2003: 241) conceptualisation of 'non-disciplinary' bio politics of the state that is subjected on the 'living man' or 'man-as-having being'. This 'politics of life' comprises of the 'power to make live and let die' where the ambiguous equilibrium between right to life and right to death is perpetually balanced in favour of death over life (ibid.). This is contrasted by Foucault (2003: 273) with the conventional articulation of sovereign authority as classical biopower which 'take[s] life or let[s] live'. Extending Foucault's notion, Mbembe (2003) conceptualises necropolitics as the 'administration of death' which showcases the ongoing patterns of subduing life to accommodate the politics of death and thereby displays the 'generalized instrumentation of human existence and material destruction of human bodies and populations' (Vajpeyi, 2009: 301). Agamben, drawing from the same body of work, has furthered the understanding of 'bare life' of 'homosacer', where the inviolability of life is adjourned and reduced to the bare minimum of human existence. The pandemic response mechanism of the state constitutes a 'state of exception' where the discriminatory and discretionary powers of the state acquire a false legitimacy in the urgency to ensure public health. When the Indian state brought about a gamut of restrictions that curtailed the right to mobility of a citizen, it was given statutory validation through the enforcement of the Disaster Management Act of 2005. All citizens of the country were subjected to the new normal of restricted mobility, denying the right to freedom of movement ensured by Article 19(d) of the Constitution. Hence the suspension of laws and rights during the pandemic exemplifies the state of exceptionality as conceptualised by Agamben (1998: 170), where 'subjective right and juridical protection no longer make any sense'. When a *citizen-migrant* to whom mobile livelihood is crucial for sustenance is subjected to this restriction as compared to other citizens for whom the same restriction would only amount to an added inconvenience in terms of limitation of choices (and not a threat for survival), it unravels the disproportionate effect of the aforementioned category of pandemic citizenship. By reducing *citizen-migrants* to the status of *homo sacer*, who is excluded from living a politically proficient life, pandemic citizenship ensures that the ambit of state protection is reduced to a mere subsistence of their bare life. In the state of exceptionality that causes 'inclusive-exclusion' or 'exclusive-inclusion' (Agamben, 2008), pandemic citizens lose the capacity to claim their 'right to have rights' (Arendt, 1986). Faced with the lack of any alternative, the pandemic citizens chose to defy the restriction when they decided to undertake a long walk home. Here biopolitics can be seen to transmute to a sort of thanatopolitics where a particular segment of the population is positioned outside the 'sphere of immunity' by the state (Esposito, 2008: 14). The death of migrant workers due to dehydration, exhaustion, hunger, and accidents in their perilous journey on foot effectively showcases the pandemic citizen as an embodiment of bare life who eventually become subjected to the thanatopolitical 'dispositif' (ibid) of the state. Thanatopolitics is then a corollary to biopolitics, where population management becomes politics of death brought about by letting some die, where death is 'elided and dismissed' as the 'necessary part of living', such that they are never 'caused' per se' rather the state merely 'allows' it to happen as a 'passive event' (Murray, 2008: 204). The lack of statistical records of the death of the migrants and the absence of any concerted attempt by the state to enumerate such deaths not just showcases the apathy towards the vulnerable but also signifies the thanatopolitical apparatus of the state that normalises the death of those excluded. It is necessary to analyse the construct of *citizen-migrant* to understand how their marginality conditions them to be expelled from the 'sphere of immunity' of the state, thereby exposing them to the viciously disproportionate impact of pandemic citizenship. The shaping of *citizen-migrant* can be zoepolitically seen as the starting point of his diminution from the politically qualified good life ('bios') to the bare and naked life (zoë) constituted by the pandemic.

The inclusive-exclusion that characterises Agamben's bare life is symptomatic of the condition of citizen-migrant where the mobility for livelihood excludes accessing rights based citizenship. Article 21 of the Indian Constitution guarantees the fundamental right to liberty, which is equivocally the right to a dignified life. Although every state is the benefactor of the right to life of its citizens both legally and politically, various patterns of exclusion relegate individuals to the margins of the body politic. This causes the right to life to be applied 'universally but not uniformally' among the citizens, triggering the state to develop 'differentiated governmental management of life' (Nasir, 2017: 76). Right to dignified life necessitates an individual's access to basic healthcare and education, and for those underprivileged languishing in peripheries of state, like the internal migrants, dignified life entails support for food rations and even livelihood assistance. Rather than conceiving citizenship as a legal status that facilitates their political and civic rights, it would be more pertinent to look at citizenship as a conduit that sanctions their social rights.

Building on T.H Marshall's conceptualisation of citizenship as a progression of civil, political, and social rights and entwining it with Arendt's notion of citizenship as the right to have rights, Somers (2008: 6) envisions citizenship as the 'foundational right' that facilitates an individual's 'social inclusion in civil society as a moral equal' and how the rights of vulnerable categories of citizens within a nation-state get degraded under the influence of market fundamentalism. Being a citizen does not automatically enable the internal migrants of the country to access the rights and entitlements accrued through citizenship, which showcases the inevitable chasm inherent between 'status and the reality of citizenship' (Houtzager & Acharya, 2011: 4). Similarly, Solinger (1993) in his study of circular migrants in China suggests that despite having legal citizenship the 'floating populations' were prevented from accessing rights and welfare provisions. To Fraser (1996), the tenets of entitlement are based on the notion of necessity for assistance, requisite of employment, and a membership in the society in terms of citizenship.[2] Though with inherent variations, most of the advanced societies hyphenate entitlements with 'definition of citizenship' premised on a 'continuous stream of income above poverty level' or a stable employment (Bakker, 1994: 6). In countries like China, the system of entitlements was conditioned by acquisition of urban residence. Interestingly, the domain of social citizenship showcases the entwinement and mutuality of political and economic rights so much so that the deprivation of one would constitute the denial of other (Roy, 2010). Chhachhi (2004), in the context of an almost non-existent framework in India to ensure the provisioning of entitlements grounded on citizenship, considers it pertinent to ascertain the overt reliability of the migrant on exchanging their labour as the primary means for subsistence.

At the outset, it is important to both locate and differentiate the precarious labour of the *citizen-migrant* within the predominant discourse of labour, in order to establish the necessity to introspect their vulnerability towards the citizenship rights of the state. Drawing on Marxian scholarship, Fraser (1996) considers disproportionate labour exchange to be a grave social injustice that involves tacit exploitation, where the benefit of one's labour is appropriated for the advantage of others, thereby constituting their economic deprivation and marginalisation. The current 'neo-liberal globalization, along with hypermobility of capital' has fortified the supply of such 'flexible labour' (Chhachhi, 2014) by feeding on the inequality emerging from such marginalisation. This must be seen in the context of erosion of the decommodification of labour in the post-Fordist era marked by the 'informalization, precariatization and fragmentation of labour' (Chhachhi, 2014: 901). The welfare capitalism that emerged during the Fordist mass production era saw the state's effort to promise a gamut of social citizenship rights that was in turn influenced by the strategies of trade union tactics and labour mobilisation. This was primarily dependent on the centrality of decommodification of labour that emboldened the worker, but also threatened the ultimate power and supremacy enjoyed by employers (Esping-Andersen, 1990: 22). The hyphenation between wage labour and social citizenship that was asserted during this period of welfare state had considerably brought down the inherent systemic inequalities and caused for a 'social levelling' (Breman & Linden, 2014; Chhachhi, 2014). The informality of the wage labour thereby challenged the hyphenation of employment with social citizenship (Barchiesi, 2008) such that it was the nature of the employment (formal/informal) which was coupled with the realisation of social citizenship. Chhachhi (2014: 903) opines that the bivalent narrative of labour that centres on the Marxian notion of 'exploitation' and Polanyian theorisation of 'commodification' can be contested by the Global South in the context of their uniqueness in terms of the development of working class under the influence of colonialism, relevance of various types of labour, entwinement of migration with labour, the function of post-colonial state, as well as the confrontation and struggle that workers underwent to attain both work-related and social rights. In alignment with postulations of other scholarship (Linden, 2008; Mezzadra, 2012; Chakrabarty, 2001), she opines that the labour question in post-colonial countries like India should recognise the categorisation of novel configurations of labour such as 'precariat, cybertariat, care workers, etc.', and the ways in which this reconfigures the class divide in the milieu of prevalent procedures and patterns of capital accumulation.

In spite of participating in the accretion of capital, the 'reserve army of labour' is structurally conditioned to be the perpetually deprived (Breman, 2013) and characteristically compared to the 'precariat'. While reconceptualising the notion of 'labour' based on the distinctions of nature of work, labour power, and distinguishing the modes of income, Standing (2011) posits the emergence of a new labour class that he calls the 'precariat' characterised by the distinctive features of uncertainty and elasticity of occupation, overt dependability on the apprehensive and flexible wages coming from undertaking such employment and the negligible realisation of substantive citizenship rights. Unlike the proletariat, they cannot be located specifically in the hierarchy of Marxist class relations in the context of capitalist patterns of production. While the prognosis and diagnosis of the proletariat question is conditioned specifically by the need to attain a sustainable protection of labour within the place of employment that, in turn, can be affiliated or associated with (such as a factory), it cannot be the same for the precariat. The vulnerability of the circular migrant labour in India that qualifies them to be the precariat in terms of their mobile livelihood and diverse skill set also precludes them to develop long-term affiliation with a particular place or segment of employment. The solution for the precariat's uncertainty and vulnerability cannot be confined to their employment but rather should be simultaneously sought outside those limits of the place of their employment. It is here that one can approach the exclusion of the precarious migrant labour by reconciling both their economic vulnerability and their political existence. By building on the Polanyian theorisation and by emphasising the inadequacy of 'industrial citizenship', Standing (2009) had put forth the necessity to re-problematise the dominant approach by supporting the de-hyphenation of employment with social citizenship and advocating 'occupational citizenship' that associates all occupations with equal rights, recognition, and identity. This can prevent the alienation of the labourer arising from mass commodification of the post-neoliberal world order. Arguably, the variations brought about in the nature of labour invoke categorisations like the precariat that warrant a realignment in introspection by combining the need to secure 'labour rights vis-à-vis capital' (Chhachhi, 2014: 903) that necessitates locating rights as the citizens of the state.

Citizenship is about accessing the resources apportioned to the citizens as much as it denotes their social membership in a community (Turner, 1990). Through making claims on the state for the resources and rights that they are entitled to, individuals are effectively 'practicing citizenship' (Kruks-Wisner, 2019: 8). According to scholarship like Lister (2000) and Molyneux (2000), the conception of 'citizenship in practice' requires a shift in the focus of citizenship as a 'process' rather than a 'status'. The question of exercising agency, whether at an individual level or at a collective level is instrumental while looking at citizenship as 'process' (Ong, 1991). The practice of citizenship ascertains an understanding on active citizenship as conceptualised by Houztager and Acharya (2011: 3), where citizens attempt to traverse the conditions for their access to public goods and provisions through exercising their agency 'in ways that are publicly sanctioned and protected'. Kruks-Wisner (2019) examines the notion of active citizenship by modifying the ways exerted by an individual to access the public goods and provisions, wherein a citizen could use both formal and informal, publicly sanctioned and even unsanctioned means to claim rights. This reclamation of rights substantively denotes the participatory notion of citizenship where an individual exerts his political agency (Lister, 1998:228). In the absence of an institutionalised state structure that proactively implements the constitutionally guaranteed rights and welfare provisions, despite being the bearer of those rights, the migrant worker faces impediments in exerting his agency and claiming those rights. Kruks-Wisner (2019: 9) opines that claim-making hyphenates two aspects of citizenship – citizenship as a status that bestows the civil, political, and social rights and the status of citizenship acquired by the individual through their participation in the political community. Going back to Somers (2008), one can see the amalgamation of these two aspects where she conceptualises the legality of citizenship rights as emanating from the impact of social mobilisation in turn conditioned by the same rights. If citizenship can be conceived as a bundle of rights to be allocated and duties, passive citizens would comprise the base while active citizenship would constitute progressively higher echelons of the hierarchy. The precarity of migrant labour is that their compounded structural exclusion conjures a gap which is in turn constituted by both the spatial bias of our citizenship rights and the migrant's mobility.

Mobile populations constitute the 'imperceptible lot' to the political leadership of our country, working in towns and cities of their home states renders them incapable to cast votes in the villages where they are electorally registered. Notwithstanding the numbers, they lack a concerted political weight due to their inefficacy in comprising the 'vote bank'. For the same reason, the working conditions, health care and housing provisions of these labourers do not figure as a pressing concern for the politicians at the places to which they have migrated for employment. The 'political disenfranchisement of circular labour migrants' (Roy, 2016) is central to their political exclusion. The disparity in the enumeration of migrants as visible in census reports and National Sample Surveys is rather too trivial a matter for the state, considering the haphazard and ambiguous definitions used to even qualify someone as migrant within the country. The ill-informed policy-making of state on internal migrants not just overlooks but also deeply discounts the economic value of the labour they undertake, as a larger number of temporary/seasonal/circular migrants remain invisible.

The way in which their workplaces are spatially dispersed across various geographical locations (Ghosh & Bandyopadhyay, 2020), the nature of complicated subcontracting provisions, and even the sheer circumstantial variety of low skilled and unskilled occupations in the country make their static settlement in one location impossible, making the 'floating population' in the suburbs and urban locations of the country. The collective mobilisation of the migrant labour so as to assert their rights or negotiate their political demands is very difficult. One cannot attribute this lack of collective assertion among the migrant workers completely to the informal nature of their work; Agarwala (2013) opines that close to nine million informal workers participate in a union, even though they lack formal working conditions. A combination of both informal employment and mobile livelihood precipitate the structural vulnerability of migrant labour in India. In addition, their inherent socio-cultural diversity in terms of the identity markers such as language, religion, or caste renders their collective organisation as a homogenous group rather challenging. The faultlines of caste, class, and gender and the diversity of their inherent skill set have constituted hierarchies of labour. The migrant labour of the country comprises largely those who belong to the lowermost levels of this hierarchy (Shah & Lerche,

2020). The nature of contractual labour recruitment for low skilled and semi-skilled jobs adds on to this complex hierarchical structure, where the migrant labour is prevented from accruing any tangible capital or resources and is perpetually subjected to the exploitation by middlemen in selling their labour.

The socio-economic susceptibility of the migrant labour is characterised by the repetitive abnegation of their social rights where affordable housing, healthcare, basic education becomes inaccessible to them due to the invisible fissures in administrative design and institutional framework of distributing the welfare provisions of the state. Srivastava (2020) outlines four factors for continued precarity of migrant labour in India – first is their inability to establish a 'civic identity and civic citizenship' at the destination, second is the unfavourable terms of assimilation to the labour market when compared to the non-migrants, third being the weak social network pattern amongst the migrants, and finally the inherent complexity in ascertaining claims and entitlements such as shelter. The inability can be attributed primarily to the lack of prior experience in exercising their citizenship rights even at their place of origin. This precludes them from developing awareness on the prerequisite of necessary documentation that would make them eligible for the entitlements and sometimes they would not know the provisions or entitlements for which they are eligible in the first place. In a complex administrative and institutional arrangement of welfare system, though money for the scheme might be sanctioned by the central government, their pattern and implementation design can vary from state to state, making it difficult for the labourer to move from his state of origin to the state of his employment to claim his entitlements from the state. The primary impediment in accessing welfare provisions is establishing their legal identity at address of domicile as identification systems like UIDAI currently can link an individual with only one address, making it difficult for seasonal and circular migrants to access the entitlements through a single address. Even the admissibility to be included in the target population of schemes such as Ayushman Bharat, P.M Awas Yojana, and National Food Security Act are determined on the basis of Socio-Economic Caste Census (SECC) updated every ten years. Except for the possibility of some being included in the state of their origin, the chances for SECC being inclusive of short-term migrants at any place are significantly less, in turn causing them to be excluded from being a targeted beneficiary for such assistance. Statutory provisions include the Inter-State Migrant Workmen (Regulation of Employment and Conditions of Service) Act of 1979, which was brought about by acknowledging the inadequacy of existing legal framework in protecting the interests of migrant workers in the country. It recognised the necessity to protect the large section of unorganised and illiterate workers from the vagaries of their informal work condition and exploitation at the hands of contracting middlemen (Varma, 2020). The structural vulnerability and socio-economic deprivation has rendered them frail to exert the agency required for claiming their constitutional rights. The awareness and adequate understanding on the implementation of a statutory law for alleviating their exploitation at work is in principle a long haul. The attempt to bridge the lacunae in existing labour laws led to the introduction of Occupational Safety, Health and Working Conditions Code of 2019 in Lok Sabha in 2019,[3] which also failed to achieve its stated purpose.

The political exclusion, marginalisation in acquiring a valid legal identity, and inability to access their entitlements create a precarious existence amidst their material hardships and socio-economic vulnerability. Such deprivation of their substantive rights and entitlements along with 'othering' that they face in the host societies can be considered to be the materialisation of an 'eclipsed citizenship' (Mander et al., 2019). Beyond the normal dichotomy of insider/outsider to the construct of citizenship, they opine that differential practices of membership within the nation-state causes some to be privileged as being 'interior' and others as 'exterior'. The plight of the migrant labour is not just that he is an outsider to the state to which he migrated but also that he is 'exterior' to the states from which he has migrated. The compounded structural exclusion has turned the migrant labour to a lesser citizen of the body politic even in the pre-pandemic normality, and curtailing the mobility of people has been central to the response measures adopted by means of complete or partial lockdown and border closures. It is at this juncture that the notion of 'politics of mobility' has resulted in 'pandemic citizenship'. Dobusch and Kreissl (2020) have opined that the nature in which states handle the response measures for COVID-19 can be likened to the way in which the crisis management transmutes as 'im-/mobility governance'. As a person's mobility is what enables him to access his livelihood or sustaining his societal and personal relations, it is inextricably linked to the constitution and reconstitution of power relations within the society (Cresswell, 2010) and thereby emerges as the 'most coveted stratifying factor' (Bauman, 1998). The statutory and non-statutory provisions intended to enable or curtail the mobility and thereby the partaking of individuals across various aspects of life ensures the disproportionate endowment of mobility along the pre-existing faultlines of class, religion, ethnicity, or even gender. For a pandemic crisis where mobility-induced proximity of individuals is the primary causative factor, the curtailment of the very same mobility emerging as the principal response mechanism of the state was perceived to be fairly just. But the implementation of such response mechanisms exhibits the inequalities and asymmetric power relations that forfeit the rights of the individual. The state meted out a visibly differential and viciously disparate treatment to migrant labour within the country in comparison to the effort and enthusiasm invested in the implementation of the Vande Bharat mission conceived so as to bring home the emigrant community from Middle East who were literally crucial to the inward remittance received by the southern states of India, like Kerala. Instead, the improvisation of state-dictated norms of mobility using haphazard categorisations such as 'stranded migrants' failed to comprehend the diverse nature of the predicament of migrant labour, resulting in the reduction of individuals to graded bodies in which some citizens are more unequal than others. The pandemic reconstituted them as potential carriers of the virus, thus making the migrant labourer an 'outsider' or 'other' who can be thanatopolitically left to die than let to live.

When citizen-migrants are subjected to a *pandemic citizenship*, it conjures a 'contrast medium' that amplifies and reveals the 'ills that affect our society'.[4] Their plight ought to be seen from the intersection of 'process, agency, and multidimensionality of exclusion', all of which create a situation of 'thwarted citizenship' (Roy, 2010: 176). The transition of migrant labour in India to a *citizen-migrant* to a *pandemic citizen* is marred with the masking, assertion, dispossession, and re-assertion of his agency. The economic marginalisation emanating from the informality of his labour and the compounded socio-political exclusion conditioned by his mobility had caused the state to precipitate structural conditions that masked him from exerting his agency required for the practice of citizenship. A *citizen-migrant* is already a lesser, unequal citizen who was included and later excluded at the same time. Baubock (2011: 3) in conceptualising 'partial citizens' describes temporary migrants as those who could not partake in the political sphere for making the same laws that they were being subjected to and whose membership status is jeopardised by the 'automatic acquisition or loss or as a result of mere change of residence' along with the absence of a robust spatial affiliation that prevents them from 'justifying fuller set of rights or motivating fuller participation'. The acquisition of livelihood is an exercise of their right to mobility, through which the migrant labour asserts limited agency. Overlooking of vulnerability and marginalisation by the state by means of imposition of a uniform blanket ban on mobility constitutes a *pandemic citizenship*, i.e., one that completely dispossessed the *citizen-migrant* of any agency to a dignified life. As opined by Roy (2010: 26–27), migrants who have been ousted from the 'elite domain of civil society' for their incapacity to manoeuver the 'skills' required for citizenship are thereby perpetually condoned to the inferior realm of 'residual citizens'. The analogy of pandemic citizen to *homo sacer* signifies how being cast out to the peripheries of citizenship exposes one to the bare life, where abstract biological life is constituted by a state of exception. Had these vulnerable people been able to access at least their basic food ration through the Public Distribution System at their areas of domicile, the migrant exodus and consequent cataclysm that we witness today could have been averted to a certain degree. When the *citizen-migrants* who are citizens deprived of substantive citizenship become *pandemic citizens*, they face a complete absence of choice, such that they are reduced to the naked life of the *homo sacer*. By defying the restrictions imposed by the state, when they set out on barefoot for a 'long march' back home, they reassert agency for a dignified life. This exposes them to the state's dichotomous choice of worthy citizens over the other insignificant citizens whose death are overtly or covertly instigated by the thanatopolitical practices of the state facilitated by the pandemic 'state of exception'. Their death both literally and metaphorically signifies the process of exclusion of the citizen-migrant culminating as the erasure of pandemic citizen.

Conclusion

To sum up, the compounded exclusion of migrants manifested by their mobile livelihood puts them into a flux between their state of origin and state of destination, which is juxtaposed against the spatial bias inherent both in our citizenship framework and the institutionalisation of our welfare provisions. These factors cause the migrant body to transmute to the *citizen-migrant* as lesser, unequal citizen unable to claim entitlements, disempowered to access rights. Agamben (2020) opines that response mechanism of the state during pandemic is the manifestation of the predisposition of the state to use a 'state of exception as the normal paradigm of the government'. The reduction of individuals to their bare life of mere biological existence devoid of any social and political dimension is normalised and accepted in fear of survival (ibid.). The state of exception and politics of mobility instituted by the state during pandemic creates the *pandemic citizen* who has forfeited his claim to the indispensable right of mobility. Yet the structural vulnerability that has constituted the citizen-migrants in the first place has made them most vulnerable to the adverse and disproportionate impact of this pandemic citizenship, reducing them to the disposition of *homo sacer* leading a 'bare life'. For the citizen-migrants, in the absence of an effective social security net and welfare provisions, their assertion of agency to be mobile is the only factor that enables them to earn the remuneration in return for the labour they engage in. While for any other citizen the constraints on mobility have only limited their choices and options in day-to-day life, the state has deprived the *citizen-migrant* of their only choice and means to a dignified life. The partaking of state in constituting their vulnerability as citizen-migrants and later as pandemic citizens becomes thanatopolitical in the way it facilitated life for the equal citizens and death to the unequal citizen-migrant. The blatant disregard for their structural predicament will cause the normality of the post-pandemic society to be built on the edifice of the very same unequal pandemic citizenship.

Notes

1 The term *pandemic citizen* has been adapted from the article 'The biopolitics of pandemic citizenship' by Adil Hossain (2020) but conceptualized differently from the original version.
2 Cross cited from Chhachhi (2004).
3 https://www.prsindia.org/billtrack/occupational-safety-health-and-working-c onditions-code-2.
4 Cross cited from Dobusch and Kreissl (2020).

References

Agamben, Giorgio, 1998. *Homo Sacer: Sovereign Power and Bare Life*. Translated by Daniel Heller-Roazen. Stanford: Stanford University Press.
Agamben, G., 2008. *The Kingdom and the Glory*. Homo Sacer II. Buenos Aires: Adriana Hidalgo.
Agamben, Giorgio, 2020. 'The Invention of an Epidemic', https://www.journal-psychoanalysis.eu/coronavirus-and-philosophers/; originally published in Italian on Quodlibet.
Agarwala, Rina, 2013. *Informal Labour, Formal Politics and Dignified Discontent in India*. Cambridge: Cambridge University Press.
Arendt, Hannah, 1986. *The Origins of Totalitarianism*. London: Andre Deutsch.
Bakker, Isabella, 1994. *The Strategic Silence: Gender and Economic Policy*. London: Zed Book Company/The North-South Institute.
Barchiesi, Franco, 2008. 'Hybrid Social Citizenship and the Normative Centrality of Wage Labor in Post-Apartheid South Africa', *Mediations*, 24(1): 52–67.
Bauböck, Rainer, 2011. 'Temporary migrants, partial citizenship and hypermigration', *Critical Review of International Social and Political Philosophy*, 14(5): 665–693.
Bauman, Zygmunt, 1998. *Globalization: The Human Consequences*. New York: Columbia University Press.
Bauman, Zygmunt, 2000. *Liquid Modernity*. Cambridge: Polity Press.
Breman, Jan, 2013. *At Work in the Informal Economy of India: A Perspective from Bottom Up*. New Delhi: Oxford University Press.
Breman, Jan and Van der Linden, Marcel, 2014. 'Informalizing the economy: the return of the social question at a global level', *Development and Change*, 45: 920–940.
Chakrabarty, Dipesh, 2001. *Provincializing Europe*. Princeton, NJ: Princeton University Press.

Chhachhi, Amrita, 2004. *Eroding Citizenship: Gender and Labour in Contemporary India*. PHD Thesis, Amsterdam Institute for Social Science Research, University of Amsterdam.

Chhachhi, Amrita, 2014. 'Introduction: the 'Labour Question' in Contemporary Capitalism', *Development and Change*, 45: 895–919.

Cresswell, Tim, 2010. 'Towards a politics of mobility', *Environment and Planning D: Society and Space*, 28(1), 17–31.

Dobusch, Laura and Kreissl, Katharina, 2020. 'Privilege and burden of im/mobility governance: on the reinforcement of inequalities during a pandemic lockdown', *Gender Work & Organizations*, 27(5): 709–716.

Esping-Andersen, Gosta, 1990. *The Three Worlds of Welfare Capitalism*. Princeton, NJ: Princeton University Press.

Esposito, Roberto, 2008. *Bíos: Biopolitics and Philosophy*. Translated by Timothy Campbell. London: University of Minnesota Press.

Foucault, Michel, 2003. 'Society Must Be Defended', *Lectures at the Collège de France, 1975–76*. Trans. David Macey, Ed. Arnold I. Davidson. New York: Picador.

Fraser, Nancy, 1996. *Social Justice in the Age of Identity Politics: Redistribution, Recognition, and Participation*. The Tanner Lectures on Human Values, Stanford University April 30–May 2.

Ghosh, Shreya and Bandyopadhyay, Ritajyoti, 2020. 'Postal Ballot voting rights: the only way migrant workers can make their presence felt', *Wire*, 21 May. Retrieved from https://thewire.in/rights/postal-ballot-votes-migrant-workers. Accessed on 16 October 2020.

Hossain, Adil, 2020. 'The biopolitics of pandemic citizenship', *Discover Society*, 11 May. https://discoversociety.org/2020/05/11/the-biopolitics-of-pandemic-citizenship/. Accessed on 11 January 2021.

Houtzager Peter, P. and Acharya, Arnab, 2011. 'Associations, Active Citizenship and Quality of Democracy in Brazil and Mexico', *Theory and Society*, 40(1): 4–5.

Kruks-Wisner, Gabrielle, 2019. *Claiming the State: Active Citizenship and Social Welfare in Rural India*. Cambridge: Cambridge University Press.

Lister, Ruth, 1998. 'Citizen in action: citizenship and community development in a Northern Ireland context', *Community Development Journal*, 33(3): 226–235.

Lister, R., 2000. 'Strategies for social inclusion: promoting social cohesion or social justice?' *Social Inclusion, Possibilities and Tensions*. Eds. Askonas, P. and Stewart, A. Basingstoke: Macmillan, 37–58.

Mander, Harsh, Roy, I. Priyanka Jain, Ravi Raman, Rashmi Guha Ray, Anirban Bhattacharya and Usman Jawed Siddiqi, 2019. 'Stolen citizenship, stolen freedoms Locating the rights of India's circular labour migrants', *Slaveries & Post-Slaveries, Open Edition Journals*. Retrieved from http://journals.openediti on.org/slaveries/602. Accessed on 16 October 2020.

Mbembe, Achille, 2003. 'Necropolitics', *Public Culture*, 15(1): 11–40.

Mezzadra, Sandro, 2012. 'How many histories of labor? Towards a theory of postcolonial capitalism', *Post Colonial Studies*, 14(2): 151–170.

Molyneux, Maxine, 2000. *Women's Movements in International Perspective*, Ed. Molyneux. Palgrave Macmillan.

Murray, Stuart J., 2008. 'Thanatopolitics: reading in agamben a rejoinder to biopolitical life', *Communication and Critical/Cultural Studies*, 5(2): 203–207.

Nasir, Muhammed Ali, 2017. 'Biopolitics, Thanatopolitics and the Right to Life', *Theory, Culture & Society*, 34(1): 75–95.

Ong, Aihwa, 1991. 'The Gender and Labor Politics of Postmodernity', *Annual Review of Anthropology*, 20: 279–309.

Roy, Anupama, 2010. *Mapping Citizenship in India*. New Delhi: Oxford University Press.

Roy, Indrajit, 2016. 'Enhancing mobility: political and social rights for circular labour migrants', *Policy Brief, No. 34112*, 1–6.

Shah, Alpa and Lerche, Jens, 2020. 'Migration and the invisible economies of care: production, social reproduction and seasonal migrant labour in India', *Transactions of the Institute of Geographers*, 2020: 1– 16. https://doi.org/10 .1111/tran.12401.

Solinger, Dorothy J., 1993. 'China's transients and the state: a form of civil society?', *Politics & Society*, 21(1): 91–122.

Somers, M.R., 2008. *Genealogies of Citizenship: Markets, Statelessness and the Right to Have Rights*. Cambridge: Cambridge University Press.

Srivastava, Ravi, 2020. 'Vulnerable Internal Migrants in India and Portability of Social Security and Entitlements', *Centre for Employment Studies Working Paper Series WP02/2020*, Institute for Human Development, Delhi.

Standing, Guy, 2009. *Work After Globalization: Building Occupational Citizenship*. Cheltenham: Edward Elgar.

Standing, Guy, 2011. *The Precariat: The New Dangerous Class*. London: Bloomsbury Academic.

Turner, Bryan, 1990. 'Outline of a theory of citizenship', *Sociology*, 24(2): 189–217.

Vajpeyi, Ananya, 2009. 'A history of caste in South Asia: from pre-colonial polity to bio-political state', in Islamoglu, Huri and Perdue, Peter C. eds. *Shared Histories of Modernity: China, India and the Ottoman Empire*. New Delhi: Routledge, 298–320.

Van der Linden, Marcel, 2008. *Workers of the World: Essays Toward a Global Labour History*. Leiden: Brill.

Varma, Satvik, 2020. 'Why India's Legal and Labour System needs to be Reconfigured to really help Migrant Workers', *Wire*, 19 May. Retrieved from https://thewire.in/labour/india-labour-legal-system-migrant-workers. Accessed on 16 October.

4 Juridicalising justice?

COVID-19, citizenship claims, and courts

Kalpana Kannabiran and
Sreekar Aechuri

Introduction

Since March 2020, India has been under a lockdown owing to the COVID-19. In what was perhaps the 'harshest coronavirus lockdown in the world', this governmental measure saw an outpouring of workers from cities and towns they had migrated to in search of work, back to their native villages that they had left in search of better lives and survival with dignity. The turbulent waves of internally displaced persons (IDPs) on the highways and railway tracks heading back 'home' will remain an enduring image of the pandemic in India. As Upendra Baxi notes, 'we must fully know the existential horror reflected in their social biographies: the economic, social and political conditions and contexts which make people move from the domicile of birth to the domicile (of their necessitous and precarious) "choice"' (Baxi, 2020a). Brahma Prakash reflects on the spectre of internal displacement and the forced return of workers to villages they had left: 'The problem of migrant workers', he observes pertinently, 'is not to be defined in terms of a choice between village and city. It is about a condition in which they are neither part of the village, nor part of the city', for we cannot afford to forget that migration of Dalits and other oppressed castes and classes out of villages is forced by the inhuman conditions in villages and the routine indignities they are forced to bear (Prakash, 2020). With worksites shut down, schools and colleges closed, curfew in place, hospitals and medical facilities ill-equipped to deal with the crisis on hand, governance floundered and rested on a series of arbitrary measures and hasty ordinances, with citizens as mere spectators and victims of the unfolding tragedy. Under the circumstances, the judiciary was the only check on the government and courts the only resort available to petitioners in urgent need of proactive intervention that was needed to protect and safeguard Article 21 rights under the Constitution – to use Justice PK Goswami's words, 'last resort of the bewildered and the oppressed'.[1]

In the context of COVID-19, Upendra Baxi underscores the importance of the 'peremptory jus cogens' that categorically set out state obligations and goes on to observe, 'only new forms of human compassion and solidarity can help overcome this lethal and formidably grim challenge and [help build] a new future for global politics marked by empathy, fraternity, justice, and rights' (Baxi, 2020b).

In this chapter, we examine the cascading jurisprudence that sprang up from the lockdown, and reflect on trends in judicial deliberations and their implications for an understanding of justice and rights under the Constitution. The rights of internally displaced persons during the lockdown and the forced migration that it triggered needs to be understood as constitutive of the understanding of justice under the 'triadic ethical framework of the Constitution'.[2]

While arbitrary state action was a major issue in the declaration of lockdown as well as in state measures at containment for the most part (Kannabiran, 2020), broadly speaking, citizens petitioned the courts on (a) the right to health and (b) rights of internally displaced persons. Apart from the specific cases brought before the courts, there were concerns raised in the media about the unprecedented surveillance on citizens in the name of containment measures (Aarogya Setu and policing practices) and the dismantling of labour protections by some state governments in the immediate aftermath of the lockdown as a way of safeguarding employers' interests.

Of particular interest is the direction in which jurisprudence has proceeded. To anticipate our argument, courts have engaged with these petitions either with deference to executive or by urging the executive to think of better policy-making instead of discussing rights, fundamental freedoms, guarantees, and their enforcement. Except for one order of the Telangana High Court, the ruling of the Supreme Court in *Puttaswamy vs. Union of India* in the matter of the non-negotiability of fundamental rights has not been cited in any of the cases pertaining to/arising from COVID-19.[3] What is the place of the Preamble and the Directive Principles of State Policy in understanding and evaluating 'COVID-19 jurisprudence'? (Kannabiran, 2021). If, as Justice DY Chandrachud says, 'it is the Constitution that is lynched when a person is lynched',[4] the deaths due to hunger, train/road accidents, physical exhaustion, custodial torture (which includes exposure to infection in custody), and custodial murders imperil the Constitution and its futures.

The right to health

In considering issues around access to health care as a core element in justice claims, it is important to look at the entire range of concerns around the right to health as also health care access specific to the pandemic. Since COVID-19 is our point of departure in this chapter, it is important to point to the demands the pandemic places on the health care system, in order to then move to the ways in which these demands have impacted on non-COVID health care needs, and then situate the specific ways in which courts have over five months addressed right to health concerns, as part of Article 21 rights. While we have several documents, studies, and statements put out by various health rights collectives in the country, we draw from Srivatsan's mapping of the pandemic in relation to institutionalised health care in Telangana state (Srivatsan, 2020). Pointing to the fact that in its fifth month, India is witnessing a full-blown community spread of COVID-19 in several states of the country, he estimates that in Telangana alone the cumulative mortality rate from COVID-19 will be over 57,000, with 90 per cent of those dying over 60 years of age. With 239,000 infected individuals seeking hospitalisation, the numbers of available hospital beds in private and public facilities falls far short – if pooled together, his estimates point to 99,919 beds. Similarly, while the requirement for ICU units is around 43,000, available units (for the most part concentrated in private hospitals) total about 5,000 in the state. There is little reason to assume a vastly different scenario in most of the other states. This then has an immediate impact on health care access for other emergency and critical cases. Anoo Bhuyan underscores the struggles of those with chronic illnesses unrelated to COVID-19 to access health care, emergency services, and affordable medicines (Bhuyan, 2020). Alongside this, triggered by the lockdown, health care needs of the exodus of workers and IDPs with no money, food, or shelter suffering deep trauma after being locked out and dispossessed in four hours, hunger, exhaustion, and utter neglect remain unaddressed. This is the largest section of people who do not enter the account of even trying to access institutionalised health care. Deaths – countless – in these cases are not counted as deaths caused by the novel coronavirus. They are also not deaths or morbidities caused by lack of access to care for chronic ailments, nor are their needs counted as critical health care needs. Where then does this aspect of COVID-19 morbidity and mortality figure in our accounts of the right to health and the right to life? This is the backdrop against which the jurisprudence on health care access during COVID-19 needs to be situated.

Although there were reports of pregnant women being turned away from hospitals and dying during or immediately after childbirth[5] and countless women being deprived access to contraceptives in line with the advisory of Ministry of Health to suspend provisions of sterilisations and IUCDs,[6] the cases that drew the attention/ire of the courts were few. Addressing this urgent need to resolve questions of reproductive justice for women, Sama, a women's health collective in Delhi, petitioned the Delhi High Court in April

2020, asking for reliefs against the denial of basic health care, and delivery and childbirth services to pregnant women and the barriers faced by families in accessing maternal health care access.[7] Despite detailed guidelines issued by the Ministry of Health and Family Welfare, Government of India, for the delivery of essential medical services – which include reproductive services, treatment for communicable diseases, chronic diseases and emergencies, health care workers, particularly Auxiliary Nurse Midwives and Asha workers – these were unavailable on the ground for the care of pregnant women. In this case, the petitioners' demand for a dedicated helpline, provision of transportation services and access to health workers for pregnant women was agreed to by the ministry, which was also putting in place a helpline for senior citizens. This is especially relevant in the light of the observation of the Gujarat High Court:

> Ordinarily, the High Court would not interfere with the functioning of the State Government. The Court steps in by mandamus when the State fails to perform its duty. The true test of an efficient Government can be determined from its performance in times like the present one.
>
> In difficult times, it is expected of any Government to rise to the occasion and protect its citizens … All that we are doing is to remind the State Government of its constitutional obligations and the directive policies of the State. In such circumstances, we expect the State Government to accept our orders passed in the Public Interest in the right spirit bearing in mind the paramount consideration of the health and wellbeing of the people as imperatively implicit in the right to life guaranteed under Article 21 of the Constitution of India.[8]

In exercising oversight over governmental measures for reining in private hospitals, increasing the number of treatment and care facilities available, providing facilities for doctors and medical personnel, taking over hotels for expansion of medical services, controlling costs and pricing by private facilities and demanding detailed reports from the government, forcing convergence between different departments, the Gujarat High Court, in response to a slew of petitions filed before the court on governmental neglect, addressed itself to the remit of the court in matters of emergency such as one triggered by COVID-19, and directed the state government to fulfil its obligations to the people under Part IV of the Constitution, recognising that 'Public Interest Litigation is meant for the benefit of the lost and lonely and of those whose social backwardness is the reason for no access to the Court' (para 53). The Telangana High Court, similarly passed orders 'in the nature of Writ of Mandamus', directing the state to report on quarantine facilities for returning international travellers, non-provision of

PPE to doctors, medical and para-medical personnel, non-availability of N-95 masks and sanitisers for the public at large, non-availability of daily essential goods at reasonable prices to the general public, and the absence of any provision for livelihood support, shelter, and protection for IDPs, homeless, students evicted from hostels, and itinerant communities, and inadequate testing facilities for COVID-19.[9] Problems of short supply of medicines, beds, and medical care leading to exploitation especially by private hospitals forced some states to cap prices related to medical treatment of COVID-19 with one of the first states – Maharashtra deciding on 22 May 2020.[10] Despite the Supreme Court's direction to the centre to ensure prices are capped in private hospitals across the country,[11] only around 12 states complied,[12] without any serious enforcement of the same with serious instances of exploitation by private hospitals persisting.[13] In looking at testing policy, and asking Indian Council for Medical Research to be impleaded, the Gujarat High Court recalled the observation of the Supreme Court in *Navtej Johar & Ors. Vs. Union of India*:

> The jurisprudence of this Court, in recognizing the right to health and access to medical care, demonstrates the crucial distinction between negative and positive obligations. Article 21 does not impose upon the State only negative obligations not to act in such a way as to interfere with the right to health. This Court also has the power to impose positive obligations upon the State to take measures to provide adequate resources or access to treatment facilities to secure effective enjoyment of the right to health.
>
> (para 28, 42/2020)

What we witness in the case of Gujarat and Telangana, for instance, is the effective opening out of the jurisprudence of 'continuing mandamus' – 'a process by which the constitutional court instead of delivering a conclusive verdict, keeps the litigation ongoing, giving orders from time to time, monitoring governmental compliance through regular hearings' (Poddar and Nahar, 2017). The important aspect of 'continuing mandamus' is of course the fact that state action on each of the problems addressed in these sweeping orders falls woefully short, forcing citizens to approach courts that may then force accountability on the government. In Telangana state especially, the sharp observations of the court and its stringent directions point to the utter inadequacy of state action that is self-driven and bound by constitutional obligations.[14] In cases where 'continuing mandamus' is the approach of the courts, there is an implicit recognition by the courts of the need to closely monitor state compliance to constitutional obligations through the entire duration of the crisis. Gautam Bhatia points towards an inter-reading of Article 14 with the right to health in his discussion on the Supreme Court's interim orders on free testing for COVID-19:

> the question is not whether a Court order interferes with the budget and is therefore illegitimate, but whether the Court order does or does not enforce a constitutional right. If it does, then the impact on the budget is a collateral issue … In the present case, therefore, the key issues are twofold: what rights are at play (… these are the rights to equality read with the right to health), and whether lack of access to testing constitutes an infringement of these rights (… the nature of the coronavirus pandemic is such that it does).[15]

We also see, in these cases, the interconnections between right to health and other Article 21 rights that, strictly speaking, may be delineated in distinct ways but cannot be disaggregated from the whole. This still limits the reach of measures to health care seekers. How many of the hundreds of thousands of IDPs – women and men – were able to effectively access health care, and how their health care needs remained unaddressed and subservient to a surveillant focus on their forced travels is a problem we must grapple with.

Rights of internally displaced persons

Any attempt to grasp and bear witness to the pandemic exodus 'must fully know the existential horror reflected in their social biographies: the economic, social, and political conditions and contexts which make people move from the domicile of birth to the domicile (of their necessitous and precarious) "choice"' (Baxi, 2020a).[16] As Deshpande and Ramachandran suggest, 'the incidence of the disease is not class-neutral: poorer and economically vulnerable populations are more likely to contract the virus as well as to die from it', and the 'economic consequences of the current pandemic are likely to be concentrated most on low wage earners' (Deshpande and Ramachandran, 2020). Examining employment data for India pertaining to April 2020, they find that the rise in unemployment immediately after the imposition of lockdown was far steeper for the scheduled castes and scheduled tribes than for the upper castes. This correlated with their earlier work of disparities in educational attainment by social group suggests again that it is the scheduled castes and scheduled tribes that faced the job losses, being concentrated in insecure precarious employment.

The question that we will examine in this section is whether, in the framing of its jurisprudence on the COVID exodus, the constitutional court was in fact cognisant of the gravity of the infringement of constitutional rights in the very imposition of lockdown as evident from its consequences. The focus, therefore, is not as much on what specific reliefs the courts ordered on but how they framed this grant/denial (as the case may be) of reliefs. This holds important lessons for our future understanding on constitutional jurisprudence on forced migration in India, and the framing of state responsibility in this situation.

Within a week of the imposition of Lockdown 1.0, the very first order passed in the matter of two petitions before the Supreme Court of India on 31 March 2020 by Chief Justice SA Bobde and Justice L Nageswara Rao is instructive in its framing of the forced migration triggered by the union government. The petitions, the court recounts,

> highlighted the plight of thousands of migrant labourers who along with their families were walking hundreds of kilometres from their work place to their villages/towns. The concern of the Petitioners pertains to the welfare of the migrant labourers. They are seeking a direction to the authorities to shift the migrant labourers to government shelter homes/accommodations and provide them with basic amenities like food, clean drinking water, medicines, etc.[17]

The court then proceeds to detail at length the *Status Report* filed by the union government in response to the petitioners' concerns: the various steps to prevent the spread of corona virus; 'various other measures … dealing with the needs of *lower strata of society*' (emphasis added); relief package of Rs. 1.70 lakh crore under Pradhan Mantri Garib Kalyan Yojana; 'the exodus of migrant labourers was triggered due to panic created by some fake/misleading news and social media;' '[t]he very idea of lock down was to ensure that the virus would not spread. It was felt [by the government] that transportation of migrant labourers would aggravate the problem of spread of the Virus; on 31 March 2020, 21,064 relief camps had been set up, 6,66,291 persons were provided shelter and 22,88,279 persons were provided food.'

In presenting its status report, the government of India sought directions from the Supreme Court to (a) issue directions for compliance by state governments of advisories issued by union government and (b) 'prevent fake and inaccurate reporting whether intended or not, either by electronic print or social medial which will cause panic in the society'.

The Supreme Court declared that it was satisfied with the steps reported by the union government to contain the spread of the virus, and in considering the situation of the exodus of workers, it went on to quote the director general of the WHO:

> We are not just fighting an epidemic; we are fighting an infodemic. Fake news spreads faster and more easily than this virus, and is just as dangerous.

There was no attempt at this stage by the Supreme Court to arrive at an independent assessment of the situation unfolding on the ground, nor was there any attempt to engage with questions of proportionality, forced displacement, forced migration, the question of dignity, and the possibilities of an exercise of continuing mandamus demanding specific performance of constitutional obligations by the state. The focus on 'stopping the spread of the virus' rendered the suffering that the lockdown unleashed opaque from the institutions of justice in the immediate aftermath. The deflection of attention from those forcibly displaced to the diversionary rhetoric of 'fake news' undermined processes of justice in fundamental ways. The second petitioner in this case, Harsh Mander, in his rejoinder to the Status Report filed by the state, pointed importantly to the problematic reliance of the court on the status report alone in its response to the matters raised in the petitions, both filed on the basis of a detailed ground report and on-site assessment of predicament of pandemic IDPs.[18] This rejoinder details the specific problems faced by the ousted workers and their families (including children), the inadequacy of the relief mentioned in the status report, the inaccessibility of the Public Distribution System (PDS) to most workers who had migrated in search of work owing to the domicile requirement of the PDS, the total exclusion of workers in the unorganised sector, notably construction workers to any manner of relief, and the deaths of workers and kin within the first week of lockdown owing to the disproportionate hardships imposed on them. The response of the court in this matter was telling, with Chief Justice SA Bobde going on record to ask the petitioner *'why wages are required when meals are provided by the government.'*[19]

This one statement by itself frames the approach of the Supreme Court of India to the Lockdown IDP's right to citizenship claims and dignity, as also its approach to questions of empathy (on its own part and on the part of the state), compassion, and fraternity in the face of grave harms and disproportionate suffering.

Although the exodus began the night that the lockdown was imposed, the fact that hundreds of thousands of the country's workers were on the road trekking infinite distances on the highways with their children and meagre belongings, no destination in sight, weeks on end, with no food or water, some dying of exhaustion, others in road accidents, others mowed down by trains while governments watched and barricaded state borders or abandoned workers at borders or sprayed bleach on returning workers, resulted in some scattered orders from different courts for 'stranded workers'.[20] Finally, the Shramik trains that yet again did not match the numbers who needed to travel across the length and breadth of the network of the Indian Railways, apart from lacking in basic facilities and schedules that were widely known and understood by those who needed to travel, prompted the NHRC to take suo motu notice and observe,

> A train getting late due to bad weather etc. for some hours is always considered beyond control of the authorities but trains getting lost during journey, reaching unexpected destinations and taking more than a week to reach its scheduled station is hard to believe and require a thorough investigation into the matter.[21]

A few states, including Gujarat, announced police action if migrants were to travel back to their states,[22] while the Karnataka government cancelled 'Shramik Trains' on a representation from the builders' association so that the displaced workers could now be put to work on construction sites.[23] This stands in stark contrast to the state of Kerala which set up a model containment and logistic policy that dealt with every aspect of the pandemic and the lockdown.[24]

Courts did go as far as to observe that the migrants 'are not afraid of COVID but they are afraid they would die due to starvation',[25] and food supply and glucose was provided in a few instances on highways.[26] The IDPs were not *afraid* of starvation, they were *dying* of starvation, and suffering from hunger. Yet, the reason for their predicament remains unacknowledged both by states and courts. In response to an Interlocutory Application seeking directions from the Supreme Court to District Magistrates to identify and transport migrants on highways within their jurisdiction to their home states,[27] Justice L. Nageshwara Rao's nonchalant observation, 'How can we stop them from walking? It is impossible for this Court to monitor who is walking and who is not walking',[28] and Justice SK Kaul's retort, 'Will you go and implement government directives? We will give you a special pass and you go and check',[29] point to a total absence of epistemic humility and judicial compassion in the face of suffering.

The jurisprudence of continuing mandamus that evolved quite quickly in several courts with respect to medical treatment, and access to health facilities, did not figure at all in the jurisprudence on forced migration induced by the lockdown. The reliefs granted by courts in the matter of IDPs, whether related to food, work, wages, or transport, remained episodic and piecemeal over three months of the lockdowns. This has to do, we suggest, with the question of class – the description for instance of IDPs as 'lower strata of society' or the Supreme Court's doubt about why workers needed wages if they were given food, put into stark relief the class-caste biases embedded in the juridicalisation of the rights of forced migrants by constitutional courts and the limitation of those rights to state largesse.

Finally, on the question of labour rights – the lockdown IDPs were all workers – ostensibly in a bid to revive the economy and incentivise local businesses and foreign investors, the states of Uttar Pradesh, Madhya Pradesh, and Gujarat, among others, exercised their powers under Factories Act, 1948, and other laws and issued notifications 'relaxing' labour laws.[30] Some of the effects of such relaxations would be extension of work hours to 12 hours a day (without over-time wages), deprivation of access to raise disputes under Industrial Disputes Act, and relaxation of measures on safety and hygiene in factories (ironically during a health crisis), among others that constitute a serious derogation of basic standards of fair labour practice and dignity of labour. Two PILs filed in the Supreme Court challenged the vires of the proposed notifications and exercise of power as violative of the Constitution.[31] The petitioners argued that such relaxation would constitute forced labour and is in violation of India's commitments to international human rights guarantees.

In relation to the question of labour protections, especially, we witness the rise of concerted coercive practices by the state – both directly and through the absence of due diligence – especially in relation to workers: forced displacement aggravated by forced labour proscribed under Article 23 of the Constitution of India.

Conclusion: Unravelling arbitrary state action

In conclusion, we dwell briefly on the subject of arbitrary state action and judicial empathy during this time. In assessing the principle of proportionality of any specific state action, disparities in access and disproportionate impact owing to social vulnerabilities are critical determining factors of 'manifest arbitrariness' – with first measures requiring safety mechanisms to be put in place to ensure minimal adverse impact on the precariat.

An important concern that figured significantly in judicial discourse which we have not been able to address at any length is the communalisation of pandemic vulnerabilities and the surge in 'genocidal journalism' in India.[32] The refusal by the Supreme Court to restrain the media from inciting hatred against Muslims[33] despite the violation of Rule 6 of Cable Television Network Rules, 1994 (which prohibits attacks on religions which promote communal attitudes), points to the earlier issue we raised about class and caste biases embedded in the juridicalisation of the pandemic, that were fundamentally majoritarian.

There were important countermoves from the Madras High Court and the High Court of Bombay in cases related to the Tablighi Jamaat meeting. The Madras High Court observed in the matter of the detention of Bangladeshi and Indonesian nationals who attended the Tablighi Jamaat congregation that

COVID-19 should teach us to care for each other rather than use the arsenal of law. Merely because the petitioners have contravened the visa conditions, they cannot be seen as criminals. The situation calls for empathy and understanding.

(para 16)[34]

The Bombay High Court observed:

> There was big propaganda in print media and electronic media against the foreigners ... There was virtually persecution [emphasis added] against these foreigners ... A political Government tries to find the scapegoat when there is pandemic or calamity and the circumstances show that there is probability that these foreigners were chosen to make them scapegoats ... It is now high time for the concerned to repent about this action taken against the foreigners and to take some positive steps to repair the damage done by such action.[35]

Can there be a sharper indictment of the government? And yet, the refusal of courts and governments to intervene to stop incitement in media points to the expanding field of impunity under a majoritarian state.

On the subject of impunity, while the spike in state impunity through custodial torture and death with numbers ranging over 7,000 custodial deaths in the period 2014–2018[36] is alarming and predates the lockdown, the use of lockdown and restricted mobility to bolster custodial torture (including wilful exposure to COVID-19 in jails where political prisoners are detained) is especially a cause for concern. State violence on civilians 'violating' restrictions on mobility (such as the custodial murder of Jeyaraj and Bennix in Sattankulam in Tamil Nadu), curbing any congregation of protest against state violence as routinely witnessed in Kashmir, and the routine and aggravated derailment of due process rights in matters of life, liberty, and dignity, as we witness in the case of the detention of a rape survivor and her counsellors in Araria in Bihar, mark the lockdown, making it a more serious human rights concern than the pandemic itself.

Public health emergencies have necessitated stringent measures of containment by states at different times in recent history, particularly through the imposition of restrictions on liberty such as quarantine, self-isolation, lockdowns, curfews, and mandatory distancing norms. However, it is precisely at times such as this that international human rights standards force obligations on states to be attentive to the limitations necessary on these drastic measures (Kannabiran, 2020). The place of empathy, transparency, and setting out blueprints of positive, enabling, non-coercive measures of containment, care, treatment, and remedies can scarcely be understated in a situation where the certainty that the overwhelming majority of persons affected will be the precariat.

In a rare (perhaps singular) expression of judicial empathy and humility, Justice G.R. Swaminathan observes,

> I feel sensitive to the petitioners' misery particularly in these pandemic times. I posed a question to myself if I am acting beyond jurisdiction? … If I come to the conclusion that the petitioners have already suffered enough and that they are being put to 'surplus or unnecessary suffering', I am obliged to intervene.
>
> (paras 17–18)[37]

A close examination of 'COVID-19 jurisprudence' (Kannabiran, 2021) points to an uneven and inconsistent focus by courts – with continuing mandamus invoked by a few courts for monitoring state action on the right to health, and an episodic, inadequate response to forced migration and displacement triggered by an arbitrary lockdown. In the blanket announcement of lockdown, the ends of justice and indeed its obligation towards the triadic ethical framework of the Constitution, especially state obligations under Part IV, were jettisoned by the state in stark ways that were manifestly arbitrary both in the means (the process) and the end (the measure).

Notes

1 *State of Rajasthan & Ors. v. Union of India*, 1977 AIR 1361.
2 Justice B. Sudershan Reddy in *Reliance Natural Resources Ltd. v. Reliance Industries Ltd.*, [2010] 156 *Comp Cas* 455 (SC).
3 *Ganta Jai Kumar vs. State of Telangana and Others*. Writ Petition (PIL) 75 of 2020 dated 25.05.2020. *Puttaswamy and Others vs. Union of India* (2017) 10 SCC 1.
4 Justice D.Y. Chandrachud, 'Why constitution matters', at: https://www.youtube.com/watch?v=vr1Dc_-ZKbQ (last accessed 27 August 2020).
5 H.S. Shreyas, 'Turned away by two hospitals, MP woman dies after delivery', *Times of India*, 24 April 2020 among other reports.
6 'COVID-19 lockdown deprives over 2 crore couples from availing contraceptives', *The New Indian Express*, 9 May 2020.
7 *SAMA-Resource Group for Women and Health v. Union of India & Ors.*, W.P.(C) No. 2983 of 2020 & CM APP Nos.10345-46 of 2020 dt, 22 April 2020.
8 *Suo Motu v. State of Gujarat*, W.P. No. 42 of 2020, *LiveLaw*, at: https://www.livelaw.in/top-stories/dont-politicize-covid-19-crisis-gujarat-hc-157618 (last accessed 27 August 2020).
9 High Court of Telangana, Common Order on W.P. (PIL) Nos. 59, 78, 81, 82 & 92 of 2020 dt. May 26, 2020; *Ganta Jai Kumar vs. State of Telangana and Others*. Writ Petition (PIL) 75 of 2020 dated 25.05.2020.

50 *Kalpana Kannabiran and Sreekar Aechuri*

10 'COVID-19 treatment: Maharashtra caps per day private hospital charges', *Mumbai Mirror*, at: https://mumbaimirror.indiatimes.com/coronavirus/news/covid-19-treatment-maharashtra-caps-per-day-private-hospital-charges/articleshow/75884756.cms (last accessed 27 August 2020).

11 'Coronavirus: SC directs Centre to cap cost of treatment at private hospitals as cases cross 9 lakh', *Scroll.in*, at: https://scroll.in/latest/967415/coronavirus-there-will-be-no-return-to-old-normal-for-the-foreseeable-future-warns-who (last accessed 27 August 2020).

12 Anoo Bhuyan, '"Exorbitant" coronavirus treatment prices slashed as state govts step up', *Business Standard*, 9 August 2020.

13 Akshita Saxena, 'Former Law Minister (Sr Adv) Ashwani Kumar writes to CJI to take Suo Moto action against reported incidents of manhandling of Covid patients/dead bodies', *LiveLaw*, at: https://www.livelaw.in/top-stories/former-law-minister-sr-adv-ashwani-kumar-writes-to-cji-to-take-suo-moto-action-against-reported-incidents-of-manhandling-of-covid-patients-dead-bodies-read-letter-158113 (last accessed 27 August 2020).

14 The Supreme Court in its suo motu order called out the governments of Delhi, Maharashtra, Gujarat, Tamil Nadu, and West Bengal for mismanagement and mishandling of dead bodies and patients shuttling around in search of testing facilities and beds, when hospital occupancy showed availability of vacant beds. *In Re The Proper Treatment of COVID 19 Patients and Dignified Handling of Dead Bodies in the Hospitals*, Suo Moto W.P. No. 07 of 2020, *LiveLaw*, at: https://www.livelaw.in/top-stories/sc-notice-to-delhi-maharashtra-tamil-nadu-west-bengal-covid-19-management-158220 (last accessed 27 August 2020).

15 Gautam Bhatia, 'Coronavirus and the constitution – XVII: The Supreme Court's free testing order – some concluding remarks', *Indian Constitutional Law and Philosophy*, at: https://indconlawphil.wordpress.com/2020/04/11/coronavirus-and-the-constitution-xvii-the-supreme-courts-free-testing-order-some-concluding-remarks/ (last accessed 27 August 2020).

16 Upendra Baxi's insistence on unpacking the opaque category of 'migrants' mindful of the important distinctions between various kinds of voluntary and involuntary, free and forced migration is extremely important in understanding the exodus that India witnessed from the end of March 2020 (Baxi, 2020a).

17 *Alakh Alok Srivastava v. Union of India*, W.P.(C) No. 468 of 2020.

18 *Harsh Mander & Anr v. Union of India*, W.P. (C) Diary No. 10801 of 2020.

19 Shruti Mahajan, 'Migrant Workers' plight during coronavirus lockdown: Will not interfere in government decision for few days, CJI SA Bobde', *Bar and Bench*, at: https://www.barandbench.com/news/litigation/migrant-workers-plight-during-coronavirus-lockdown-will-not-interfere-in-government-decision-for-few-days-cji-sa-bobde (last accessed 27 August 2020). Emphasis added.

20 *Prof. Rama Shankarnarayan Melkote v. State of Telangana*, W.P. (PIL) No. 94 of 2020.

21 'Trains getting lost, reaching unexpected destinations require thorough investigation': NHRC takes Suo Moto notice of migrants' hardships in Shramik trains', *LiveLaw*, at: https://www.livelaw.in/top-stories/nhrc-takes-suo-moto-notice-of-migrants-hardships-in-shramik-trains-157488?infinitescroll=1 (last accessed 27 August 2020) and other similar stories.

22 'Coronavirus: Travel and face police action, Gujarat warns migrant workers', *The Hindu*, 27 March 2020; Rashid, Omar, 'Coronavirus lockdown: U.P. police warning against helping migrants sparks row', *The Hindu*, 15 May 2020.

23 https://thewire.in/government/karnataka-trains-migrant-workers (last accessed 27 August 2020).

24 Kerala's description of workers from other states as 'guest workers', however, remains deeply problematic and counter-constitutional in terms of the freedoms allowed to all citizens to move and settle within the country under Article 19 of the Constitution.

25 *Suo Moto v. State of Gujarat*, W.P. No. 42 of 2020, order dt. May 11, 2020, *LiveLaw*, at: https://www.livelaw.in/top-stories/gujarat-hc-takes-suo-moto-noti ce-of-lockdown-miseries-of-hungry-migrant-workers-covid19-lockdown-156 635 (last accessed 27 August 2020).

26 *Ramakrishna v. UoI*, W.P. No. 101 of 2020, *LiveLaw*, at: https://www.livelaw.in/ top-stories/migrants-crisis-ap-hc-says-if-court-doesnt-react-it-would-be-failing -in-its-role-issues-slew-of-directions-156865 (last accessed 27 August 2020); *Suo Moto v. State of Gujarat*, W.P. No. 42 of 2020.

27 *supra* note 17.

28 Radhika Roy, '"How can we stop them from walking?"': SC refuses to entertain plea for migrants on road', *LiveLaw*, at: https://www.livelaw.in/top-stories/sc-re fuses-to-entertain-plea-for-migrants-on-road-156803#:~:text=The%20Suprem e%20Court%20on%20Friday,16%20migrant%20labourers%20in%20Aura ngabad. (last accessed 27 August 2020).

29 *Id.*

30 The Supreme Court of India struck down the Gujarat notification in a judge-ment delivered on 1 October 2020 in *Gujarat Mazdoor Sabha and Anr v. State of Gujarat*, Writ Petition (Civil) No. 708 of 2020. For a detailed discussion see Kannabiran (2021).

31 Articles 14, 15, 19, 21, 23, 38, 39, 42, 43-A and 47. Roy, Radhika, '"State depriving oppressed classes of welfare": Plea in SC challenges dilution of labour laws by Gujarat, UP & MP', *LiveLaw*, at: https://www.livelaw.in/top -stories/plea-in-sc-challenges-dilution-of-labour-laws-by-gujarat-up-mp-15 6771 (last accessed August 27, 2020); Akshita Saxena, 'Labour without wel-fare measures constitutes "Forced Labour" under article 23 of constitution: Plea in SC against dilution of labour laws', *LiveLaw*, at: https://www.livelaw. in/top-stories/labour-without-welfare-measures-constitutes-forced-labour-un der-article-23-of-constitution-plea-in-sc-157057 (last accessed 27 August 2020).

32 Suchitra Vijayan, 'Journalism as genocide', *The Wire*, at: https://thewire.in/c ommunalism/journalism-as-genocide (last accessed 27 August 2020).

33 Sanya Talwar, '"Cannot Gag the Press": CJI on plea seeking action against some media houses for communalising coronavirus pandemic', *LiveLaw*, at: https:/ /www.livelaw.in/top-stories/cannot-gag-the-press-cji-on-plea-seeking-action -against-media-houses-for-communalising-coronavirus-pandemic-155177 (last accessed 27 August 2020).

34 *Kamerul Islam and Ors vs. The State*. CRL OP(MD)Nos.5769, 6018 & 6103 of 2020. Madurai Bench of Madras High Court. 12 June 2020, ordering the release of Bangladeshi and Indonesian nationals detained in jails in Tamil Nadu after attending the Tablighi Jamaat congregation.

35 *Konan Kodio & Ors v. State of Maharashtra*, W.P. (Cri.) No. 548 of 2020, *LiveLaw*, at: https://www.livelaw.in/news-updates/bombay-hc-says-tablighi-jamaat-foreigners-were-made-scapegoats-quashes-firs-against-them-criticizes -media-propaganda-161793 (last accessed 27 August 2020).

36 '4 years – 7085 deaths in police and judicial custody', *Project 39A*, at: https://
twitter.com/P39A_nlud/status/1285079471880409090 (last accessed 27 August
2020).
37 *Supra* note 33.

References

Baxi, Upendra, 2020a. 'Exodus Constitutionalism', *The India Forum*, 29 June.
Retrieved from https://www.theindiaforum.in/article/exodus-constitutionalism.
Accessed on 12 October 2020.
Baxi, Upendra, 2020b. 'Nations Must Not Ignore Principles of Existing International
Law in Fight Against COVID-19', *The Indian Express*, 10 April.
Bhuyan, Anoo, 2020. 'How Healthcare Became Unaffordable for Non-COVID
Patients During the Pandemic', 19 June. Retrieved from https://www.indiaspe
nd.com/how-healthcare-became-unaffordable-for-non-covid-patients-during-the
-pandemic/. Accessed on 12 October 2020.
Deshpande, Ashwini and Rajesh Ramachandran, 2020. 'Differential Impact of
COVID-19 and the Lockdown', *The Hindu*, 22 August.
Kannabiran, Kalpana, 2020. 'Rights and Justice in Viral Contexts in India', *The
India Forum*, 01 May. Retrieved from https://www.theindiaforum.in/article/jus
tice-and-rights-viral-contexts-india. Accessed on 12 October 2020.
Kannabiran, Kalpana, 2021. 'COVID-19 Jurisprudence: Triadic Ethical Framework
and the Faultlines of Constitutional Governance', In Bandyopadhyay, Ritajyoti,
Banerjee, Paula, Samaddar, Ranabir (eds.), *Covid-19 and Migrant Workers*. New
Delhi: Social Science Press; New York: Routledge, forthcoming.
Poddar, Mihika and Bhavya Nahar, 2017. '"Continuing Mandamus": A Judicial
Innovation to Bridge the Right-Remedy Gap,' 10 *NUJS L(Rev)*.
Prakash, Brahma, 2020. 'Why I Won't Live in My Village and Won't Leave the City
Till Forced to,' *Outlook*, 28 July.
Srivatsan, R., 2020. 'How Should We Prepare for the COVID 19 Health Crisis in
Telangana?' Retrieved from https://www.anveshi.org.in/wp-content/uploads
/2020/07/How-should-we-prepare-for-the-COVID-19-health-crisis-in-Telan
gana.pdf. Accessed on 12 October 2020.

5 The 'new normal'

Making sense of women migrants' encounter with COVID-19 in India

Indu Agnihotri and Asha Hans

Introduction

The COVID-19 context

> This pandemic is deeply hurting the economic interests and well-being of our nation's middle class, lower-middle class, and poor segments. In such a time of crisis, I request the business world and high-income segments of society to as much as possible, look after the economic interests of all the people who provide them services.[1]

These words by the prime minister in the run-up to the lockdown as a first step towards dealing with COVID-19 raised many hopes. This was despite the fact that COVID-19 effectively descended on India with a deafening silence, ushered in by a stringent lockdown imposed at barely four hours' notice towards the end of March 2020. However, the quiet was soon shattered by a growing demand by migrant workers for food, shelter, and transport. The most powerful images were of women and men with headloads, without footwear and bleeding feet, and a woman dead on a platform with a child trying to wake her. These visuals briefly turned the gaze on to a hitherto unrecognised reality: the existence of millions of internal migrants – homeless, invisible, and unrecognised, on whose intense labour the story of India's double-digit growth has for long been written.

The presence of the absence: Official response to migrant women's needs

The Government of India (henceforth GOI) started to respond to the migrant crisis with executive decisions which were, not surprisingly, insensitive to gender needs. Starting 27 March 2020, several orders were issued by the

GOI to curb movement of migrants who, faced with loss of work and no income to meet their daily food requirements, had no option but to throng to railway stations and bus stands or hit the highways, in an effort to return to their homes/source areas. GOI, meanwhile, called on States and Union Territories to take 'strict measures' to prevent the exodus, laying stress on the need to '*prevent any disruption to law and order*' (GOI, 2020, emphasis added). In the meantime, under the Pradhan Mantri Garib Kalyan Yojana (PMGKY) food and minimal cash were offered to convince the migrant workers and homeless people to stay where they were. Purportedly aired over the public address system, the orders went unheeded, as hundreds of thousands of migrants, including women who, dependent on daily earnings for immediate survival needs, set out on foot, laying bare the unpreparedness of the state to handle the crisis. On 29 March 2020, the Ministry of Home Affairs, GOI issued an order that this movement of large number of migrants in some parts of the country was a violation of the lockdown measures on maintaining social distancing. States were again directed to ensure adequate arrangements for food and shelter, 'to mitigate the economic hardship of the migrant workers', while also proclaiming that 'all the employers … shall make payments of wages at their workplace on the due date, without any deduction, for the period of closure during the lockdown'. Landlords too were directed not to 'demand payment of rent for a period of one month', with forceful vacation of rented accommodation or hostel premises being liable for action under the Disaster Management Act (GOI, 2020a). A quick read of the orders issued indicates that there was no recognition of specific needs or gendered vulnerabilities.

Official responses, even as they referred to 'stranded migrants', remained frozen in the frame of maintaining 'law and order'. These failed to accord dignity to men and women, whose hard labour had significantly contributed to the profits of the corporate world. The visible absence of women in the notifications pointed to a policy that did not address any women's specific needs, leave alone take cognizance of their rights. The contrast was there for all to see: stay at home orders flying in the face with thousands of migrants out on the streets; starvation, disease, and death stalked them on their homeward journeys, even as deaths due to COVID-19 continued to increase.

This chapter contextualises recent developments within the longer histories of issues concerning gendered migration (Centre for Women's Development Studies, 2012; Sansristi [Hans and Patel], 2006-2007, Patel and Hans, 2017). It pulls together selections from available evidence to argue that the marginalisation of women in the discourse on migration effectively aims at the denial of dignity and human rights to migrant workers, while it simultaneously reinforces gender norms and stereotypes. The obliteration from public view of the experiences of migrant women workers – be they brick-kiln or sugarcane workers in rural and peri-urban India; garment or domestic workers in urban locations – allows for evading difficult questions with regard to narratives of the neoliberal paradigm. Narratives of migrant women's lives, captured in studies, point to precarity and increasing vulnerabilities, with food and livelihood security emerging as critical in the face of colossal job and income losses. True, individual stories of women's and young girls' courage and resilience continue to be highlighted by some media. Moreover, reports clearly point to the pandemic having exacerbated inequalities and raised the level of vulnerabilities. The accumulation of uncertainties and insecurities in the lives of women, combined with a visible loss of work, portend increasing violence in lives steeped in the volatility of contemporary times. Rather, emerging trends underline how the convergence of poverty, gender, and marginalisation has played out during the pandemic, to render women, and specific categories amongst them, especially vulnerable.

Central to the chapter is a concern that the discourse on migration remains affixed to a gendered narrative with women migrants remaining largely unrecognised or, at best, selectively 'visibilised'. To compel policy to be more accountable to feminist concerns, there is, at the same time, a need to critically examine the new vocabulary that has emerged with the outbreak of the pandemic. How does this advance an agenda wherein the nation's needs and interests are spelt out in dissonance with the everyday needs of women, putting at risk their right to a life with dignity? What are the losses labouring people, especially women, are likely to suffer with the enforcement of this 'new normal', which snuffs out channels for articulation of dissent while it condemns the working poor to a life of precarity through hastily adopted Labour Codes in pandemic times under the garb of 'labour reforms', in the name of simplifying the labour regulatory regime?

There has been a deep link between disasters, economics, and politics, but literature on this aspect is missing (Racioppi, 2016). Women in search of incomes and livelihood, facing enormous challenges in the labour market as a result of declining opportunities for work, are likely to be doubly affected. Their daily struggle to feed their families saw no end in sight. Meanwhile, with domestic workers 'locked out', their contribution to city life became visible all of a sudden, their presence often taking on a political hue, with claims being made to success in handling the pandemic. The visible lack of political will to address the governance challenges turned the health pandemic into a deep human tragedy, whose depth may not be fathomed for long years to come. The failure of the state to recognise and address the humanitarian crisis ushered in by the sudden lockdown virtually mocked at the misery of migrants and their families. The visibly stark indifference of the 'strong state' to the suffering of the masses may perhaps be the most significant learning from this pandemic.

The context and contours of women's migration

While migration has a long history, India has seen a huge increase in its scale since the adoption of neoliberal policies. This has its roots in agrarian distress, which has visibly deepened since the 1990s (Krishnaraj, 2006, Chandrasekhar and Ghosh, 2004). The lack of employment opportunities for both men and women, but more so for women, posed serious survival issues, with a growing number exiting from rural India in search of employment, often having incurred huge debts. Marked by varied short and long-term circulatory patterns, these defy classification as per usual typologies. Drawing attention to the fact that migrants fall through the cracks in the maze of clauses and conditionalities, scholars and activists have regularly pointed to the need to extend coverage of social security benefits to migrants along with portability of rights to enable them to avail of these (Srivastava, 2020). Identifying women and their specific needs within the histories and experiences of migration poses both conceptual and methodological challenges. Firstly, a mono-causal approach to data collection typically presents women's migration as being linked to reasons of marriage, despite evidence that while

> some implicit or actual labour migration by women may appear in the data as marriage migration or as other forms of associational movement by women simply because both may coincide, but the social reason is presumed to be all important. Even where women of a migrant family enter the paid or income earning workforce in their individual capacity at any given destination, it is still possible that marriage or family movement would be given as the reason for migration since the social (marriage and family) and economic (employment, business, etc.) reasons for migration are often congruent to the point of intersection in the case of women
>
> (Agnihotri et al., 2012: 18)

This bias persists despite the fact that

> the rising numbers and proportions of women migrating for work are no less striking. Census figures showed a spurt in female migration for employment and business from around 41 hundred thousand (lakhs) in 2001 to 85 hundred thousand (lakhs) in 2011, and an increased female share of such migrants from 12% to 16%. Census data also showed a shift in the pattern of female labour migration from predominantly

rural destinations to a distinctive tilt toward suburban destinations. Forty-seven percent of all women migrating for work/business were in urban areas in 2001.

(Mazumdar and Neetha, 2020: 26)

Gender work and the sexual division of labour

I am aware of the problems you have faced – some for food, some for movement from place to place … However for the sake of your country, you are fulfilling your duties.[2]

This statement needs to be read alongside the official data on women workers, most of whom fall in the unorganised sector. According to the International Labour Organization (ILO), an estimated 400 million informal sector workers are at the risk of abject poverty in India, as a result of COVID-19 (ILO, 2020). It is well known that approximately 94 per cent of women workers are in the informal sector. The Periodic Labour Force Survey 2018–2019 estimates demonstrated the enormous gap between the male and female labour force participation rate (LFPR) and in the male/ female work participation ratio (WPR) (GOI, MOSPI, 2019: 4).[3]

Alongside falling WPR, categories to measure work underestimate the contribution of women to the economy. The lack of recognition of women's contribution in the rural economy is accompanied by the disguised nature of women's employment in the brick kilns; in sugarcane cutting in Western India, and in domestic work, all sectors which have seen a significant increase in women's migration over the last decade and more. This stems from women's migration and their labour being perceived as part of a 'family' unit, both with regard to migration and the labour recruitment process. Despite increasing numbers, given the prevalent gender biases there is no recognition of their migration histories nor of their 'work', leave aside realisation of the need for gender sensitive regulatory frameworks in the specific sectors where women workers are concentrated.

The last two decades have seen an overall decline in female employment, especially in rural India and an increase in women's migration to urban areas. Women domestic workers have, in the meantime, seen an increase, with the supply of workers being maintained through a regular flow of distress migration. This work continues to be marked by informality, the absence of formal contracts, low wages, and poor bargaining conditions. An inherent flexibility tilted towards performing additional domestic work overlaps with stereotypes of gendered work and the sexual division of labour. At the same time the work remains embedded within the inequalities of caste and class, with the share of domestic workers coming from other backward classes, scheduled castes, and upper castes represented in that order (Neetha, 2019: 2–7).

Evidence collected by surveys and studies undertaken during and after the lockdown, highlights the fact that the pandemic has disproportionately affected migrant women, depriving them of opportunities to work with poor access to the schemes/welfare measures announced. A survey by the All India Democratic Women's Association (AIDWA) of over 1,700 domestic workers across 11 states found that at a disaggregated level, more than half had lost their jobs, the extent being dependent on the spread of the pandemic. Nearly 87 per cent families were without a mode of livelihood (AIDWA, 2020b: 10). Data from another survey demonstrated that during the lockdown, migrant women reported huge work loss: construction workers being the worst hit (97 per cent), home workers (91 per cent) and waste pickers (86 per cent) (ISST, 2020: Table 3).

The impact on domestic workers has to also take into account the different layers of unacknowledged burdens, as for instance, when they became sole earners with husbands having lost their jobs, the paranoia around the pandemic put them under unusual stress and also increased their domestic responsibilities (AIDWA, 2020b: 10). Care burdens during the pandemic has had a multiplier effect. Besides care of children, the elderly, and dependents with disabilities in the family, there is the added burden of family members affected by COVID-19. The pre-pandemic imbalance in gender distribution also saw an increase in unpaid work within the household. Women's care economy also affected the LFPR but without women's contribution to care work the economy would slide further.

During the pandemic the vulnerability to intersecting deprivations became more visible, with access to food and housing emerging as critical needs. Unable to access income/earnings, women and families with no other resources or assets had neither the means of survival nor any savings to counter the pandemic. Located at the intersection of social and economic inequalities, women continue to face gendered impediments to exploring their chances of securing work at all, leave alone on better terms even in regular times. Further, during the lockdown when 'paid domestic "help" was unavailable, upper-class women were easily pushed back into gendered domesticity, proving the inadequacy of paid domestic services as a solution to mundane, back-breaking household work' (John, 2020: 44–45). The pandemic exposed the faultlines in solidarities sought to be built along gender lines as also the persistence of intersectionalities across gender, caste, and class. Pre-existing inequalities along gender and caste lines are likely to get reinforced, unless the specific contours of disadvantage are recognised and addressed. In situations of severe economic shock in such contexts, women's loss of even their limited assets and indebtedness is common, as they have limited resources and little or no savings to tide over a crisis. During the pandemic women reported having to sell these limited assets, including jewellery, to pay for family needs, or to arrange for stranded husbands to catch Shramik trains or buses home (Thomas and Jayaram, 2020).

The absolute fragility of human lives – given the absence of a policy which prioritises social security for all citizens – is perhaps the single most important learning from the experience of the pandemic. The NREGA, enacted in 2005, has emerged as the pillar of hope in these months. It is imperative that steps be taken to put in place an Urban Employment Guarantee Scheme through appropriate legislative measures to address unemployment among men and women, including migrants, on a long-term basis. Also required is an administrative framework which recognises migrants' entitlements to their citizenship rights in both source and destination areas; non-surveillant regulatory measures to enable migrants to access welfare measures and schemes without making women more vulnerable; and portability of rights to address the present restrictions on access to entitlements in destination areas. The present conditionalities for benefits result in added levels of insecurity, which again have specific meaning in the lives of women. These policy interventions should be designed with a commitment to inclusion of women, especially from the marginalised social groups.

Health and food insecurity: Interlocked in a systemic exclusion

While the disease makes no distinction between people or genders, the fact is that the impact of the disease and strategies adopted to tackle it affect people in diverse ways, given the differential location, sustaining capacity, and health and financial status of the affected population. In the absence of universal health access and portage in social security systems, the pandemic hit everyone hard, with special problems being faced by migrants, of whom a large section were women. Faced with lack of money due to the sudden lockdown, thousands of migrants, women and children, were seen walking hundreds of miles to reach their homes. Babies were born on the roads, in auto-rickshaws at hospital gates, and in the Shramik trains. Deaths of mothers and new-born babies increased threefold (AIDWA, 2020a: 4). Although data on migrant women's morbidity and mortality is still not available, a study undertaken among informal workers in Delhi found that accessing transport was most difficult. This, in turn, constrained access to essential medicines and health services (ISST, 2020: Table 2). With priority being given to the pandemic, other medical services were put on hold, resulting in the lack of care for pregnant women.

Women migrant workers are known to face violence and physical injury, raising health concerns in their efforts to find work. Women in the sugarcane industry in recent years have been forced to undergo hysterectomy by contractors in collusion with the private health establishments to prevent loss of work hours due to menstruation. This has had a serious impact on the long-term health of the women as they developed issues of hormonal imbalance and mental health (Jadhav, 2019). During the pandemic this group of migrant women, with pre-existing health issues, were left out of the government schemes supposedly introduced to provide livelihood to returning migrant workers due to the COVID-19 lockdown (Kinjawadekar and Roy, 2020). Work under the MGNREGS is known to provide a survival strategy to women, even as the hard manual labour can affect their health. It is reported that with male migrants returning, women's work saw a decline (Sharma, 2020). The pandemic has, as Deshpande argues, exposed the many faultlines that lay beneath the surface which have implications for women's and children's health outcomes. In addition to being important in themselves, these have implications for women's ability to participate in paid work (Deshpande, 2020b).

For women migrants returning home, especially those pregnant, no health care services were provided. The first point of contact for the migrants on their return home were the frontline workers, specifically the ASHA and Anganwadi workers, 90 per cent of whom are women. They have been intrinsically engaged in public health outreach work during the pandemic, despite not being recognised as 'workers' and denied a regular wage. This lack of economic protection and utter disregard for female care work/workers should not be surprising in a system known for its apathy and lack of sensitivity.[4] During the present health emergency and enforced lockdown the unavailability and increased costs of such essentials for women point to a health crisis in the making (Mendoza, 2020).

Violence against migrant women is common phenomena (Hans and Patel, 2006-2007); however, during COVID-19 no data on violence is available. Violence has broad parameters, be it physical, economic, or social. Since the beginning of the pandemic, a study revealed, a majority of households (80 per cent) were consuming less food (Kesar et al., 2020: 2). Another on migrants indicated that (60 per cent) faced severe shortages in food supplies of which construction workers and waste pickers faced the highest shortages in accessing food (ISST, 2020). Less than half the domestic workers accessed dry rations from the PDS shops, while the others, forced to buy from the open market, felt the impact of increasing prices, with no visible efforts made to regulate them. Not being able to buy/provide milk for children was a new low point of the poverty visible because of the pandemic. Banks not allowing women without Aadhar cards to withdraw their own money – not a new issue – became life threatening for women at this time (Centre for Equity Studies et al., 2020: 40).

The health sector saw no clear response or strategy to fight the virus during the lockdown. The funds sanctioned were less than 0.4 per cent of the GDP (Ghosh, 2020: 6). Despite a provision for cash transfers for maternal health and institutional deliveries under the National Health Mission (NHM), the conditionalities for availing of schemes and the lack of portability, posed serious limitations with few actual benefits reaching those who needed them.

The pandemic points to the critical need to usher in policy changes to strengthen the public health care system through budgetary allocations, with special provision for women's health needs. Social security measures incorporating gender concerns in health are required. In the absence of these, the 'new normal' sought to be created in the pandemic is heavily slated against the vast majority of women, the poor, and migrants. It is imperative that policy discussions be made more gender sensitive to include the concerns of a critical mass who in all likelihood will be made to bear the social costs of the crisis.

Conclusion: The pandemic, security, and women migrants

Addressing the UN on 2 October 2020, the Indian Minister for Women and Child Development proclaimed that India had taken several measures to ensure the 'safety, security, and well-being of women during the corona virus pandemic and continuity of care of women especially pregnant, lactating and women in vulnerable situations to build a just and equal world for women and daughters in the post COVID situation' (Deshmukh, 2020). We have documented above that workers and migrants, without food or money to pay rents, required immediate relief, but the announcements by the GOI were a minimal financial support in Prime Minister Jan Dhan Yojana (PMJDY) accounts (Rs. 500) and free/subsidised ration to needy families (GOI Ministry of Finance, 2020). There has been parsimony of relief measures, despite declaration of inflated official packages (Deshpande, 2020a: 14–15, Ghosh, 2020: 4). Many migrants who did not have Aadhar (identity) cards could not access the relief.

There was also violation of GOI's 29 March 2020 order which stipulated that employers make payment of wages of their workers, at the workplace on the due date without any deduction for the period they are under closure during the lockdown (GOI, 2020a). Construction workers, including women, did not benefit from the above orders, given the ambiguity about who their 'employer' was. Despite substantial evidence, it is not officially recognised that the majority of workers in India in the organised sector are effectively informal workers with no social security benefits. Recruited through contractors, the names of a majority go unrecorded in muster rolls – allowing for the evasion of licensing procedures and denial of entitlements to social security benefits as per law. Women construction workers, living in shanties with no access to their rights to crèches, toilets, and disparity in wages and faced with a high risk of injuries, reported both widespread loss of paid work and failure to access relief announced by the Construction Workers' Welfare Board in Delhi (ISST, 2020). With the economy collapsing, the money could only have come from the government but even the Labour Departments across the country remained silent spectators to the misery of thousands of women migrant workers and their dependents exposed to suffering from 'invisible poverty' – a term which would need redefining.

Security has not been an important indicator in migrant women's protection. Analyses of migrant women's security does not imply only physical but requires our probing deep into the reactions and contradictions of the term 'security' itself. In this chapter we shift the word 'security' to 'human security', as it broadens the definition of the term. Reardon argues that human security can be achieved only when understood in equivalence with gender equality (Reardon, 2019: 7). We argue it can be used in the in the case of migrant women who face tremendous violence in different forms. We agree that our thinking of security must be transformed, and viewed in relation to women's daily lives and 'gender particularities'. The framework we propose seeks answers to women migrants' perception of security. What has been the role of the state in protecting them, whether in place of destination or at home? The human security framework[5] in the context of this chapter includes, very simply, fulfilment of the basic needs, physical security, and dignity.

Overall, this chapter brings together snippets from a rich repertoire of studies conducted under difficult circumstances during the pandemic by civil society organisations and young researchers, who struggled to generate a body of knowledge which shall allow for deeper analysis in post-pandemic times. Clearly, two issues surface in readings of these reports: food and income loss. It was not surprising that more than the pandemic itself, the fear of starvation was a major cause of stress to women since providing food is primarily seen as their responsibility. Anticipating this, women's organisations had from the start pushed for free distribution of rations and cash disbursal (AIDWA, 2020a).

COVID-19 highlights the significance of an interdisciplinary, inter-sectoral, and trans-sectional approach to understanding discrimination against women across multiple sites, in the context of neoliberal policies in India, where the state and government collude to deny women, workers, and citizens the right to equality and human dignity. Among the issues that surfaced during the pandemic, food and livelihood security emerged as critical for social development in the years to come. These also have very specific meanings in the lives of women with regard to their assigned roles in society, their aspiration for equality and a life with dignity and their special vulnerabilities. There are clear indications that the pandemic is likely to be used as a pretext to impose further constraints on democracy, given the inclination to meet the expectations of corporate capital. The stifling of free debate has resonance in the homes, for those who justify checks on democracy in the public sphere seek to also push back efforts to democratise the home/domestic environment. India is already a witness to bizarre reactions to emerging issues of mental health and familial/marital discord. The emerging political narrative seeks to assert a homogeneity and erasure of diverse familial forms, cultures, and identities – to fit them into a narrow sectarian hyper-nationalist frame. In such a context, discussions on domestic violence and autonomy are likely to be brushed aside, even as the shadow of violence which looms over the lives of women across different stages of their life cycle acquires new, deeper meanings. Violence in the lives of women, especially those from Dalit, minority, and tribal groups, remains entrenched and intertwined with structural inequalities. These constitute the social world in which women struggle to survive, confronting specifically gendered forms of oppressions. The vocabulary and architecture of strategies to deal with the pandemic signal the reinforcing of multiple exclusions, discriminations, and vulnerabilities. What meaning these will hold for women in an overall climate of heightened insecurities is a field which throws up more questions than this chapter can answer.

Notes

1 Government of India, PIB, 2020.
2 Text of prime minister's address to the nation on 14 April 2020 released by Government of India PIB 2020.
3 LFPR is at 18.6 for female compared to 55.6 for male. This gap is also reflected in the WPR which is 52.3 for males in comparison to female WPR at 17.6 per cent.
4 For example, a public request had to be made in 2018 not to tax sanitary napkins.
5 The human security framework calls for human well-being and fulfilment of four basic conditions, a life-sustaining environment, the meeting of essential physical needs, respect for identity and dignity of persons and groups, and protection from avoidable harm and expectation of remedy for unavoidable harm (Reardon and Hans, 2019: 2).

References

Agnihotri, Indu, et al, 2012. *Gender and Migration: Negotiating Rights – A Women's Movement Perspective*, New Delhi: Centre for Women's Development Studies.

AIDWA, 2020a. 'Covid-19 Pandemic and the Modi Regime: The Invisible Despair of Women'. http://aidwaonline.org/aidwa-booklet-invisible-despair-women. Accessed on 10 October 2020.

AIDWA, 2020b. *Impact of Covid-19 Lockdown on Domestic Workers in India, 24 March to 4 May 2020: Domestic Workers' Survey*, New Delhi: AIDWA.

Centre for Equity Studies, Delhi Research Group and Karwan-E-Mohabbat, 2020. 'Labouring Lives: Hunger Precarity and Despair Amid Lockdown'. http://cen treforequitystudies.org/wp-content/uploads/2020/06/Labouring-Lives-_Final-R eport.pdf. Accessed on 10 October 2020.

Centre for Women's Development Studies, 2012. *Gender and Migration: Negotiating Rights- A Women's Movement Perspective*, New Delhi: Centre for Women's Development Studies (CWDS).

Chandrasekhar, C.P. and Ghosh, Jayati, 2004. *The Market That Failed: Neoliberal Economic Reforms in India*, 2nd ed. New Delhi: Leftword Books.

Deshpande, Ashwini, 2020a. 'The Covid-19 Pandemic and Lockdown: First Order Effects on Gender Gaps in Employment and Domestic Time Use in India', *GLO Discussion Paper, No. 607*, Essen: Global Labor Organization (GLO).

Deshpande, Ashwini, 2020b. 'The Covid-19 Pandemic and Lockdown: First Effects on Gender Gaps in Employment and Domestic Work in India', *Discussion Paper Series in Economics, DP No. 30*, June, Dept of Economics, Ashoka University.

Deshmukh, Arundhati, 2020c. 'Several of Our Legislations Have Been Strong Enablers of Women Empowerment', Says Smriti Irani at UNGA. *Law Street Journal*, October 5. https://lawstreet.co/executive/several-women-empowermen t-smriti-irani-unga. Accessed on 10 October 2020.

Ghosh, Jayati, 2020. 'A Critique of the Indian Government's Response to the COVID-19 Pandemic', *Journal of Industrial and Business Economics*, 47: 519–530.

Government of India, 2020a. DO NO. 11034/01/2020-IS-IV, dt 27.3.2020 Sd/ HS.

Government of India, 2020b. DO No. 40-3/2020-DM-I (A) dt. 29 .3.2020.

Government of India (GOI), Ministry of Finance, 2020. Finance Minister announces Rs 1.70 Lakh Crore relief package under Pradhan Mantri Garib Kalyan Yojana for the poor to help them fight the battle against Corona Virus. 26 March.

Government of India, MOSPI, 2019. *Periodic Labour Force Survey (PLFS) – Annual Report July 2018 –June 2019*. http://www.mospi.nic.in/sites/default/files /press_release/Press%20Note.pdf. Accessed on 10 October 2020.

Government of India PIB, 2020. https://pib.gov.in/PressReleseDetail.aspx?PRID +1614215. Accessed on 1 September 2020.

Hans, Asha and Patel, Amrita, 2006–2007. 'Impact of Increasing Migration on Women in Orissa (Study in the Districts of Bolangir and Nuapada)', *Sansristi and National Commission for Women*. http://ncwapps.nic.in/pdfReports/NC WMigrationReportOrissa.pdf. Accessed on 12 October 2020.

International Labour Organization, 2020. *ILO Monitor: Covid-19 and the World of Work. Updated Estimates and Analysis*, 5th ed. Geneva: International Labour Organization.

ISST (Institute of Social Studies Trust), 2020. 'Impact of Covɪᴅ-19 National Lockdown On Women Informal Workers in Delhi', https://www.isstindia.org/ publications/1591186006_pub_compressed_ISST_-_Final_Impact_of_Covid _19_Lockdown_on_Women_Informal_Workers_Delhi.pdf. Accessed on 10 October 2020.

Jadhav, Radheshyam, 2019. 'Why Many Women in Maharashtra's Beed District Have No Wombs', *The Hindu Business Line*, 11 April. https://www.thehindu businessline.com/economy/agri-business/why-half-the-women-in-maharasht ras-beed-district-have-no-wombs/article26773974.ece. Accessed 5 September 2020.

John, Maya, 2020. 'Lockdown and Beyond: Domesticity and Its Substitute', *Economic and Political Weekly*, 27 July, 55: 26–27.

Kesar, S., Abraham, Rosa, Lahotia, Rahul, Nath, Paaritosh and Basole, Amit, 2020. *Pandemic, Informality and Vulnerability: Impact of* Covid-*19 On livelihoods in India*, Bengaluru; Centre for Sustainable Development, Azim Premji University.

Kinjawadekar, Mugdha and Roy, Anoushka, 2020. 'Beed and Left-out Migrants', *The Statesman*, 9 October.

Krishnaraj, Maithreyi, 2006. 'Food Security, Agrarian Crisis and Rural Livelihoods: Implications for Women', *Economic and Political Weekly*, 41(52): 5376–5388.

Mazumdar,Indrani and Neetha, N., 2020. 'Crossroads and Boundaries: Labour Migration, Trafficking and Gender', *Economic and Political Weekly*, 55, 20, 16 May, Review of Women's Studies.

Mendoza, Clarence, 2020. 'Covid-19 Lockdown: Impact on Menstrual Hygiene Management', *CNBCtv18*. https://www.cnbctv18.com/healthcare/covid-19-lockdown-impact-on-menstrual-hygiene-management-6018721.htm. Accessed on 10 October 2020.

Neetha, N., 2019. 'Introduction', In Neetha, N. (ed.), *Working at Others' Homes: The Specifics and Challenges of Paid Domestic Work*. New Delhi: Tulika.

Patel, Amrita and Hans, Asha, 2017. 'Women and Unorganized Sector A Situational Analysis of the Construction Sector in Odisha and Gender Concerns', *Sansristi and Odisha Commission for Women*, Bhubaneswar.

Racioppi, Linda. 2016 *Introduction in Linda Racioppi and Swarna Rajagopalan. Women and Disasters in South Asia: Survival, Security and Development*. London: Routledge.

Reardon, Betty A. 2019. 'Confronting the Militarized State Security Paradigm: Human Security from a Feminist Perspective' in Betty A Reardon and Asha Hans. *The Gender Imperative: Human Security vs State Security*. New York: Routledge.

Reardon, Betty A. and Hans, Asha, 2019 *Introduction Challenging Patriarchal Violence in Reardon Betty A and Asha Hans. The Gender Imperative: Human Security vs State Security*. New York: Routledge.

Sharma, Harikishen, 2020. 'Migrants Back, Women's Share in NREGS Dips to 8-year Low', *Indian Express*, 25 August.

Srivastava, R., 2020. 'Vulnerable Internal Migrants in India and Portability of Social Security and Entitlements', *IHD*. http://www.ihdindia.org › IHD-CES_WP_02_2020.

Thomas, Cenny and Jayaram, Nivedita, 2020. 'In Indian Cities, Home-Based Workers Are Being Paid Rs 15 for a Day's Work Since the Lockdown', *Scroll.in*. https://scroll.in/article/968574/in-indian-cities-home-based-workers-are-being-paid-rs-15-for-a-days-work-since-the-lockdown. Accessed on 12 October 2020.

6 The long walk towards uncertainty

The migrant dilemma in times of COVID-19

S. Irudaya Rajan, Renjini Rajagopalan, and P. Sivakumar

Introduction

The onslaught of COVID-19 thrust upon humanity two major challenges, that of human health and that of the economy; our migrants are mired in both. It has both pushed the world economic order into chaos and challenged even the mightiest of economies. The initial advent of COVID-19 sowed confusion within systems of governance as countries struggled to deal with its unprecedented threat. In order to control the spread of the infection, countries across the globe, including India, took to strictly limiting movement of the masses. This severe and unprecedented curtailment of mobility through strict lockdown made evident that the first and worst victims of the pandemic are the marginalised, the migrants.

In the context of COVID-19, rural–urban migration has attracted the most attention given that the retreat of migrants from their urban centres has been the most visible aspect of the pandemic. The pandemic has both exposed the magnitude of India's dependency upon internal migrants for low-end jobs and the vulnerabilities they face in spite of such dependency. Additionally, this is going to destabilise India's aspirations in achieving its Sustainable Development Goals (SDGs), as the country will be compelled to address poverty from scratch so as to bridge the inequities that have cropped up as a result of the pandemic. Doing so will also require us to rethink our strategies when it comes to migrant welfare and come up with both short-term measures to alleviate migrant suffering and long-term approaches that are able to address the systemic vulnerabilities and injustices.

The economic and social crisis generated by the COVID-19 pandemic is deeper and more pervasive than any other pandemic that has affected the world since the 1900s, affecting almost every sector and its workers (World

Bank, 2020b). When it came to migrant workers, the most affected section were unskilled and semiskilled migrants whose day-to-day livelihoods suddenly vanished. With many such migrants inhabiting the informal sector and working on a contractual basis, they faced the prospects of immediate termination of employment much before their formal counterparts. Many sought to go back to their villages, but the absence of transport prevented them from doing so. State governments sought to set up relief camps and shelters to accommodate migrants, but implementation was skewed. Faced with increasing economic distress and the prospect of utter destitution, many were compelled to break government norms on travel and curfew and walk hundreds of kilometres to reach their hometowns. For an unfortunate few, this ended in the tragedy of death.

This chapter briefly summarises the Indian migrant experience during COVID-19. We look at existing and ongoing labour reforms, particularly with respect to labour rights and migrant welfare. In doing so, it looks at existing and ongoing institutional reforms, particularly with respect to social welfare, labour rights, and migrant welfare, and concludes that migrant welfare needs to go beyond stop-gap arrangements towards enacting a comprehensive body of changes aimed at improving their overall circumstances.

Trends and patterns of internal migration

Migration has a history as old as humanity, and India is no exception to this. India has long been the land of the world's largest voluntary and involuntary migration (Tumbe, 2018). On the basis of geographical movements, internal migration can be classified as rural–rural, rural–urban, urban–rural, and urban–urban, while its purpose can result in migration being time-bound and seasonal, or driven by other permanent or semi-permanent factors. Each of these patterns has been catalysts for India's changing demography and deserves to be studied at depth. But the phenomenon of return migration and the possibility of remigration in the aftermath of the COVID-19 pandemic limit our focus to that of labour migration in the rural–urban context and the vulnerabilities of migrants occupying this space.

There are significant studies on internal labour migration and how it contributes to addressing poverty in low-income countries (Deshingkar, 2006; Rajan and Sumeetha, 2019). The 2030 Agenda for Sustainable Development recognises, for the very first time, the contribution of migration to sustainable development (Migration Data Portal, 2019). Dwindling livelihood opportunities, meagre wages, and limited resources thus provide impetus for rural to urban migration. However, such migrants are often handicapped by the loss of their social and cultural identities, among other things. The absence of critical skills and adequate bargaining power further compels them into exploitative environments where they are forced to engage in low-end, low-value, and hazardous work (Aajeevika Bureau, 2014).

However, government response to the phenomenon of internal migration has largely been one of apathy. A World Bank 2018 report highlights this indifference in the very documentation of migrants in India. Multiplicity of data points over years, and overlapping classifications aside, each have their own definitional shortcomings, including the incapability of adequately addressing gender concerns or certain classes of migrants such as circular or short-term migrants (Nayyar and Kim, 2018). Besides this, surveys and other data collection processes only count the respondents who affirm their presence at the time of such an exercise (Rajan et al., 2020). Invariably, it is likely that both our data and understanding of migrants are severely under-documented (Government of India, 2017).

The 2011 census data indicates that internal migration in India accounts for 37.4 per cent of the total population as compared to 31 per cent in 2001. With the total number of internal migrants in India numbering at 453.6 million in 2011, we also see a 45 per cent increase as compared to 2001. Besides the substantial increase in overall numbers, there is also considerable change in gender dimensions with regard to India's internal migration (Figure 6.1).

The unprecedented growth of million-plus cities and dwindling economic opportunities in rural areas are understood to be key factors of massive migration. According to the 2011 Census, Uttar Pradesh and Bihar are the largest source of inter-state migrants, while Maharashtra and Delhi were seen to be receiving states due to their demographic dividend (Rajan, 2013). That said, much of the migration over the last few decades seems to be intra-district migration (see Figure 6.2).

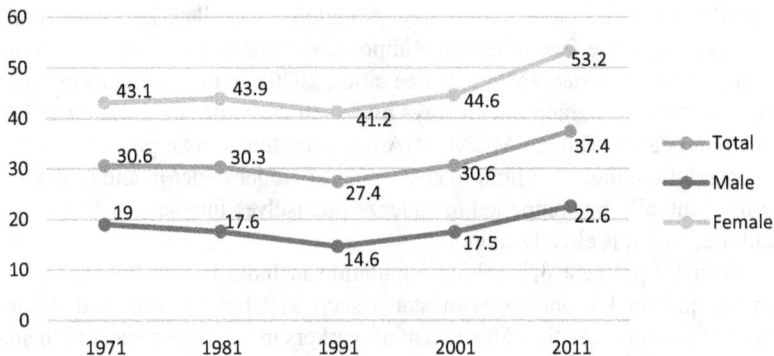

Figure 6.1 Internal migration in India, 1971–2011. *Source*: Census reports.

2001	2011

☐ Intra-district ☐ Inter state ☐ Inter district   ☐ Intra-district ☐ Inter state ☐ Inter district

Figure 6.2 Distribution of internal migrants by type of movement. *Source*: De, 2019.

A 2016 World Bank study on internal migration sheds light on this phenomenon by highlighting how despite internal mobility being a key driver of economic growth across regions, it may remain inhibited in India by the existence of state-level entitlement schemes – primarily, the inability to port social welfare measures for migrants, across state borders (Kone et al., 2017).

Migration, migrants, and the COVID-19 impact

Socio-economic impact of COVID-19 on migrants

The reverse migration generated by COVID-19 poses a massive challenge to migration governance. The problems with employment that predated the pandemic continue to remain at play with the added shock to the economy, making re-employment and income generation difficult. While many migrants remain resolute in not wanting to return back to the urban spaces that once housed them, they struggle to assimilate into their rural hometowns in the face of extreme impoverishment as well as suspicion of being COVID carriers (Migrants flee cities, 2020). In turn, officials in such rural hometowns grapple with ways by which the returning masses can be accommodated. Though MGNREGA has been touted as a possible short-term solution, there is a limit to absorption of labour under it, and migrants will eventually be compelled to squeeze themselves into sectors like agriculture, which is already saturated.

Over 90 per cent of working population in India is currently engaged in the informal economy, with states such as Uttar Pradesh and Bihar accounting for more than 80 per cent of workers in this sector, most of them migrants (Patel, 2020). For instance, Stranded Workers Action Network (SWAN) (2020) survey chronicling the hardships faced by migrant workers during the initial weeks following the lockdown saw the largest number of respondents emerge from the states of Bihar (25 per cent), Jharkhand (28 per cent), and Uttar Pradesh (13 per cent). Also, of all the Shramik trains transporting migrants operated in May, the highest were for the states of Uttar Pradesh and Bihar (Dastidar, 2020).

Investigations like SWAN (2020) highlight how migrant distress has far exceeded any relief provided. However, the pandemic has only exploited existing vulnerabilities and injustices plaguing migrants, the presence of which has been made apparent to governments well before the advent of the pandemic. Case in point is the 2017 Report by the Working Group on Migration constituted by the Ministry of Urban Housing and Poverty Alleviation, which was tasked to look into ways by which migrant welfare could be uplifted. Their report identified 53 districts (based on Census, 2001) seeing major male inter-state migration, of which 24 belonged to the state of Uttar Pradesh, followed by 20 districts from Bihar (Government of India, 2017). Yet, to-date their recommendations remain pending with the Government of India (Prabhu, 2020; Rajan and Sami, 2020); their delayed implementation will now adversely impact the dignified rehabilitation of India's migrant labour.

COVID-19, migration, and the gender lens

Migrant women have been on the frontlines of the COVID-19 pandemic, even though the public narrative about migration has been largely masculinised. Gender norms in particular prop up their own barriers when it comes to migration in the form of policy restrictions, discrimination, violence, and exploitation. Despite this, multiple women migrate internally and outside country boundaries for social, educational, and economic concerns. It is estimated that half of over 272 million migrants in 2019 who lived and worked outside their countries of origin were women, of which 66 million were migrants (Anonymous, 2020). This is true for within India too, where the primary cause of internal female migration was seen to have been marriage or associated migration (Rajan and Sivakumar, 2018), but many who did so subsequently also entered the labour force, though surveys have failed to adequately capture this (Prabhu, 2020; Rajan et al., 2020).

Gender norms and societal barriers result in women being excluded from the formal labour market, and even in an informal one, they are found at the bottom of the pyramid, employed in low-paid, insecure, and informal spaces like domestic workers, sanitation workers, and care givers. The ILO estimates the highest percentage of women (58.2 per cent) to be employed in the service sector (World Bank, 2020a) and they have been hardest hit by COVID-19 (Sharma, 2020; Sapra, 2020), putting women migrants in a far more precarious situation as compared to their male counterparts. Rukmini (2020) estimates that in India alone, within 2 months of lockdown, 4 out of every 10 working women lost their jobs, resulting in over 17 million women being rendered jobless. Despite such sizeable distress, the absence of inclusivity in the labour economy and the general lack of gender sensitive policy-making have rendered the suffering of women migrants invisible (Sapra, 2020).

Paid work aside, all other factors that constrain women in the labour force have also been exaggerated as a result of the pandemic. Women bear a disproportionate amount of the care work globally; UN Women 2015–2016 (Nandi, 2017) reveals how in India alone, women do 7 times as much unpaid work as men yet are treated as non-workers because they do not engage in work considered 'economically productive'. During COVID-19, the lockdown, coupled with social and gender norms, has forced women to put in greater number of hours into domestic labour, which run counter to social distancing norms thereby increasing their risk of contracting virus (The Week, 2020). They have also been at the receiving end of greater sexual violence as well as domestic abuse, and many report health issues due to their inability to access health, sanitation, and nutritional services due to the disruption and re-routing of, public services to fight the pandemic.

The intersectionality of migration is such that women, who are urbane and educated, and who have overcome social, economic, and gender barriers have fared better in general, and continue to do so regardless of the pandemic. But for those who are economically disenfranchised and those who belong to disadvantaged castes and communities, who form the vast majority of migrant women, the economic downturn coupled with the vagaries of working in the informal sector has rendered them far more vulnerable than they have ever been before. Experts suspect that in the aftermath of the pandemic, problems of debt, loans and mortgage will end up burdening these women, resulting in distress sales of property, child marriage, and even prostitution (Rajan et al., 2020). Unless the gendered aspect of migrant distress is recognised, and sound, inclusive, and gender-responsive policies are quickly enacted, such women will be forced to contend with a far worse exploitative environment in the new economic normal.

Institutional responses and state initiatives tackling the migrant crisis

Cognisant of the deep economic impact of the COVID-19 lockdown on the economy, the Centre quickly galvanised its resources to introduce a financial stimulus package called the Pradhan Mantri Gareeb Kalyan Yojana, which covered various categories of people from women to informal workers and many others (PIB India, 2020). It provided a combination of food support and cash transfers through existing schemes like MGNREGA, PM-KISAN Yojana, Ujjwala, etc., and leveraged institutional mechanisms like PDS and Jan Dhan bank accounts for disbursement. While these measures may have no doubt proved beneficial for those already included within such scheme ecosystems, it nevertheless proved exclusionary to low-income groups not enrolled in the existing schemes and those on the move, a large number of whom happen to be internal migrants. This realisation has resulted in the Centre augmenting these measures by way of a compendium of initiatives under the 'Atmanirbhar Bharat Abhiyaan' or Self-Reliant India initiative. However, as Iyer (2020) reports, its uptake leaves much to be desired. Attempts have also been made to collect migrant data so as to ensure their assimilation back into the workforce. The setting up of an online centralised dashboard – the 'National Migrant Information System' (NMIS) under the National Disaster Management Authority (NDMA) – to track migrant movement across states (Ministry of Home Affairs, 2020), and the proposed data bank dedicated to tribal migrant workers who are returning to their home states under the aegis of the Ministry of Tribal Affairs (Mitra, 2020), are some such efforts.

The pandemic has also forced all states, in particular those now at the receiving end of the return migration, to contend with migrant issues beyond the initial short-term rehabilitation measures of food and shelter. Faced with the possibility of long-term rehabilitation and reintegration of migrants, states have begun to undertake various measures, from collecting data on skilled and unskilled migrants (Rajasthan), to their skills mapping (Uttar Pradesh and Jharkhand), to setting up platforms and authorities to address their specific needs (the Migrant Commission in Uttar Pradesh) to online platforms to enable the skilled migrants to connect to employment opportunities (Madhya Pradesh) (Venugopal and Gaur, 2020; Srivastava, 2020; Sharan, 2020; Yadav, 2020).

That said, some of these states (Uttar Pradesh, Madhya Pradesh, Gujarat, and Rajasthan) have also diluted existing labour norms for a set time period, in an aggressive effort to reclaim economic growth and revitalise the economy, prompting fears that they will end up accommodating migrant workers in an economy devoid of basic legal protections for them (Jha, 2020; Rajan et al., 2020).

The need for social protection systems for migrants

Srivastava (2013) notes that India's labour market has long been characterised by extreme inequalities that result in the most vulnerable being subjected to high levels of livelihood insecurity, culminating in poverty and vulnerability. The Ministry of Statistics and Programme Implementation (2019) Periodic Labour Force Survey found that among regular wage/salaried employees in the non-agriculture sector over 71.1 per cent had no written job contract, 54.2 per cent were ineligible for paid leave, and 49.6 per cent did not qualify for any social security benefit.

Such inequities have become exacerbated as a result of the economic disruptions caused by the COVID-19 (Coronavirus in India, 2020). The World Bank estimates on global poverty looks at impoverishment in the aftermath of COVID-19 across the globe, and offers 'a sobering picture' for India by stating that extreme poverty is likely to remain unchanged, but that the country is expected to see more poor emerging post-COVID (Mahler et al., 2020). Juxtapose this against the latest data on how India has managed to lift approximately 273 million people out of multidimensional poverty over the last decade (UNDP & the OPHDI, 2020) and one realises that the recent economic shocks delivered to India's economy by the pandemic has the ability to derail any progress achieved over the last ten years. This includes any gains made towards attaining the Sustainable Development Goals, given how migration is a cross-cutting issue, finding relevance under targets and indicators under 11 out of 17 SDGs (Migration Data Portal, 2019).

This is where social protection, namely the ability to access it, gains importance. Enabling strong systems of social protection offers a safety net that protects the poor and the economically vulnerable from deprivation. In times of unprecedented crisis, such as the one brought about by the current COVID-19, they offer a guaranteed safety net so that migrants do not fall back into poverty.

The link between social protection and labour reforms

India has had a plethora of social safety net programmes since the early 1970s which have ranged from self-employment and wage employment programmes to food and nutrition schemes and health care. However, these programmes have traditionally sought to ameliorate deprivation via promotional measures such as offering social assistance, rather than protective ones that help deal with contingencies like health shocks, death, or disability (Sharma and Arora, 2011). More tellingly, these programmes tend to cover only those belonging to the formal and organised sectors, while an overwhelming majority of India's workforce languish in informal and irregular employment. Nowhere is this more apparent than in the nature of India's labour laws whose applicability is confined only to India's organised sector, while systematically depriving those in the informal sectors – like migrants – of the same protection.

However, India has not been entirely unaware of the need to protect informal and migrant workers. The Centre has devoted the last couple of years towards creating social security measures such as pensions (the Pradhan Mantri Shram Yogi Maan-dhan) and health insurance specifically catering to their needs, though the uptake has not been overly successful (Mitra, 2020). However, benefits of central government schemes are often tied to concepts of 'domicile', and relayed by state or local governments to those who permanently reside within their borders, thereby becoming inaccessible to inter-state migrants. Some states wilfully exclude migrants by way of domicile-based reservations in jobs, education, and service delivery (Mitra et al., 2020). However, there has been a growing recognition of the gap between how deeply entrenched migrant welfare and protection is to the space they occupy in the labour economy. Certain states like Kerala, home to migrant labour friendly policies from pre-pandemic times, with the Kerala Inter-State Migrant Workers Welfare Scheme, 2010, the Awas scheme, 2017, and the Apna Ghar Hostel Scheme, 2017, stood out for having successfully identified and housed its migrants, and securing them their entitlements during the pandemic (The Week, 2020; Rajan, 2020).

The ongoing attempts of the government to reform India's labour laws and converge them into 4 Labour Codes, in particular the introduction of the Code on Social Security 2019, must also be seen from the lens of migrant welfare. At its simplest, the Bill seeks to enhance the ambit of what constitutes a worker, and for the first time recognises categories of workers such as gig, platform, unorganised workers, freelancers, home-based, and self-employed workers as those deserving of social security measures (Ministry of Labour, 2019). Recent discussions on the Bill by the Parliamentary Standing Committee vetting the same have also made a strong pitch for improving the coverage of Employees' Provident Fund (EPF) and Employees State Insurance Corporation (ESIC) to an estimated 30 lakh migrant workers (Ray, 2020). However, critics have pointed out that efforts to broaden definitions of what constitutes a 'worker' and an 'employer' to ensure greater inclusivity have resulted in definitions that are rather ambiguous, and that the Bill does not clarify if its schemes at all extend to the unorganised sector, thereby prompting fears that migrant households might find themselves doubly excluded by virtue of being migrants (Simran et al., 2019). Therefore, social protection policies must go beyond strengthening labour norms.

Concluding remarks

The contours of what a comprehensive migrant welfare framework might look like requires a more nuanced look at migrant distress that covers various types of internal migrants as well as an in-depth inquiry into inter-sectional concerns involving various sub-categories of the migrant demo-graphics. That said, certain institutional reforms and policy interventions offer an axis from which to further future reform. An attempt has been made to briefly summarise the definitional discrepancies, suggesting robust cred-ible data collection systems, ensuring portability of social welfare, and ena-bling political franchise of migrant workers.

Existing research pinpoints discrepancies in data collection regarding internal migrants and the circumstances underlying their migration. From definitional gaps that are unable to adequately capture the nature of migra-tion such as seasonal or cyclic migration to those that ignore the eventual entry of female migrants into the labour force after marriage, there are many such concerns. This highlights a need for consistency and uniformity in the way migration is defined. One way to do this could be to appropri-ately amend migrant classifications under the Census, and use it to survey migrants across the country. This can later be leveraged by Ministries of Women and Child Development, Social Justice, and/or Minority Affairs to better their dispensation of schemes or benefits to their target audience.

While multiple surveys and research platforms – both government and otherwise – curate migrant data, they do not do so at regular timely intervals, and sample sizes greatly vary. Also, few states have been con-sistently capturing migrant data, and national estimates vary greatly from state estimates. Kerala once again stands out here since it has had the ben-efit of numerous data captures, beginning from Centre for Development Studies-Kerala Migration Surveys (Zachariah et al., 1999, 2000; Rajan and Zachariah, 2019), down to several government efforts (Narayana et al., 2013). However, it is imperative that robust, regular, and credible data col-lection that can be routinely accessed and updated be collected in a central-ised manner and in real time.

Many states have begun this enterprise now, and the Centre too has set up the National Migrant Information System to capture migrant data, though the former suffers from geographic limitations, and the latter stops at migrants repatriated back to their home states. Therefore, it is important to integrate these efforts to create a single, national online data repository that is accessible across states, into which states can feed their migrant data regularly. The ground work for such data collection can already be found in legislations like the Inter-state Migrant Workmen (Regulation of Employment and Conditions of Service) Act, 1979 (replaced by the Occupational Safety, Health and Working Conditions Code, 2020) and the Unorganized Workers' Social Security Act, 2008. However, efforts will have to be made to ensure that such a process is inclusive and captures data of those migrants who are not formally or traditionally employed.

Here, Jharkhand's method of relying on Sakhi Mandals, the state's SHG networks, to help with data capture for skills mapping offers a good example of creatively leveraging other institutional networks to help with such efforts (Bisoee, 2020). Such steps will help governments design better evidence-based welfare measures and dispense social security in a targeted fashion for migrants in the long-term. More importantly, enabling the timely collection of reliable data will also go a long way towards 'facilitating the orderly, safe, regular and responsible migration and mobility of people, including through the implementation of planned and well-managed migration policies', which is a direct target set under Goal 10 of the SDGs.

With many social protections being tied to permanent residences, migrants remain perennially outside welfare loops. Even as they hope to migrate for better economic returns, the inability to access their welfare dues outside their state of origin renders them reluctant to migrate (Kone et al., 2017). However, migration remains a key driver of economic resurgence, and in order to induce the same, it is important to dismantle administrative and other barriers that inhibit access to welfare programmes across borders. An online migrant database which is updated in real time and perhaps linked to a unique migrant number which can be cross-referenced against Aadhaar might help in this endeavour. Problems with Aadhaar verification notwithstanding, doing so might help in the more targeted dispensation of existing and proposed government benefits such as the 'Migrant Workers Welfare Fund', implementing the 'One Nation, One Ration Card' system, and enrolling migrant workers under the Ayushman Bharat scheme as well as in the potential expansion of the newly launched Garib Kalyan Rojgar Abhiyan which currently focuses only on 116 districts of the country.

The inequalities facing migrants during COVID-19 cannot be addressed without rectifying existing migrant concerns, none more so than their political disenfranchisement (Rajan et al., 2019). It is a sad reality that migrants remain an ignored category because state governments do not see themselves gaining from addressing migrant concerns. Currently political rights, namely that to vote, remain tied to permanent residences, depriving migrants off the ability to politically participate in the state they currently reside in. Granting migrants political visibility would help make their concerns take centre stage during elections. That said, the portability of political rights and particularly its ties to social welfare, is a controversial one; migrant communities are usually excluded from mainstream societies in the states they reside in, and often viewed with suspicion; therefore, enabling political franchise could also lead to parochialism. Nevertheless, political franchise remains a key enabler to migrant welfare, so states should commit to it (Aggarwal, 2019).

Migrant concerns are unique, yet they cannot be seen in isolation of other concerns plaguing the Indian economy right now. COVID-19 has not created the migrant crisis but merely made its faultlines visible. With the pandemic likely to stretch on indefinitely, future migration patterns remain uncertain, likely to intercept with reverse migration and remigration, both. What is certain, however, is the need for a paradigm shift from the piecemeal way migrant worker issues have been framed thus far. Instead, it is apparent that the crisis requires not a stop-gap arrangement but a humane, dignified, and long-term solution to address migrant needs.

***

Acknowledgements: The authors acknowledge the research contribution provided by Ms. Meghna Jayasankar. This chapter is part of a larger status paper titled 'Impact of COVID-19 on Internal Migrants in India' prepared for the UNICEF and published by Rajiv Gandhi National Institute of Youth Development, Sriperumbudur, Tamil Nadu.

References

Aajeevika, Bureau, 2014. Retrieved from http://www.aajeevika.org/labour-and -migration.php. Accessed on 27 August 2020, 12 October 2020.

Aggarwal, Varun, 2019. 'Missing migrant voters in India and why they matter; states with higher rates of migration known to have lower voter turnouts', *FirstPost*. Retrieved from https://www.firstpost.com/india/missing-migrant-voters-in-in dia-and-why-they-matter-states-with-higher-rates-of-migration-known-to-have -lower-voter-turnouts-6450361.html. Accessed on 12 October 2020.

Anonymous, 2020. 'Addressing the impacts of the covid-19 pandemic on women migrant workers', Retrieved from https://www.unwomen.org/-/media/headquar ters/attachments/sections/library/publications/2020/guidance-note-impacts-of -the-covid-19-pandemic-on-women-migrant-workers-en.pdf?la=en&vs=227. Accessed on 12 October 2020.

Bisoee, Animesh, 2020. 'Sakhis key to migrant database drive', *The Telegraph*. Retrieved from https://www.telegraphindia.com/india/coronavirus-lockdown -sakhis-key-to-migrant-database-drive/cid/1777714. Accessed on 12 October 2020.

Coronavirus in India, 2020. 'COVID-19 lockdown may cost the economy Rs 8.76 lakh crore; here's how', *Business Today*. Retrieved from https://www.business today.in/opinion/columns/coronavirus-in-india-covid-19-india-lockdown-econo my-cost-gdp-gva-nationwide-shutdown/story/399477.html. Accessed on 12 October 2020.

Dastidar, G. Avishek, 2020. 'Most Shramik trains: Gujarat, Maharashtra to UP and Bihar', *The Indian Express*. Retrieved from https://indianexpress.com/arti cle/india/most-shramik-trains-gujarat-maharashtra-to-up-and-bihar-6432299/. Accessed on 12 October 2020.

De, Supriyo, 2019. *Internal Migration in India Grows, But Inter-State Movements Remain Low*. Retrieved from https://blogs.worldbank.org/peoplemove/intern al-migration-india-grows-inter-state-movements-remain-low. Accessed on 12 October 2020.

Deshingkar, Priya, 2006. 'Internal migration, poverty and development in Asia', *ODI Briefing Paper 11*. London: Overseas Development Institute.

Government of India, 2017. *Report of the Working Group on Migration*. Ministry of Housing and Urban Poverty Alleviation.

Iyer, Kavitha, 2020. 'Falling through the holes of Atmanirbhar Bharat schemes, migrant workers seek to return to cities', *The Scroll*. Retrieved from https://sc roll.in/article/969880/falling-through-the-holes-of-atmanirbhar-bharat-schemes -migrant-workers-seek-to-return-to-cities. Accessed on 12 October 2020.

Jha, Somesh, 2020. 'Ensure that changes to Indian labour laws adhere to global standards', *Wire*. Retrieved from https://thewire.in/labour/ilo-india-labour-laws-covid-19. Accessed on 12 October 2020.

Kone, Zovanga L., Maggie Y. Liu, and Aaditya Mattoo, Caglar Ozden and Siddarth Sharma, 2017. 'Internal borders and migration in India', *World Bank Policy Research Working Paper Series 8244*. Washington.

Mahler, Daniel G., Christopher Lakner, R.A.C. Aguilar, and Haoyu Wu, 2020. *Updated Estimates of the Impact of COVID-19 on Global Poverty*. Retrieved from https://blogs.worldbank.org/opendata/updated-estimates-impact-covid-19 -global-poverty?cid=SHR_BlogSiteShare_EN_EXT. Accessed on 12 October 2020.

Migration Data Portal, 2019. *Migration & Development: Sustainable Development Goals*. Retrieved from https://migrationdataportal.org/resource/migration-deve lopment-and-evaluation-where-we-stand-today-and-why. Accessed on 30 August 2020, 12 October 2020.

Ministry of Home Affairs, 2020. *National Migrant Information System (NMIS)*. Retrieved from https://pib.gov.in/PressReleasePage.aspx?PRID=1624540. Accessed on 12 October 2020.

Ministry of Labour, 2019. *The Code on Social Security, 2019*. Government of India.

Ministry of Statistics & Programme Implementation, 2019. *Periodic Labour Force Survey 2017–8*. Retrieved from http://www.mospi.gov.in/sites/default/files/p ublication_reports/Annual%20Report%2C%20PLFS%202017-18_31052019.p df. Accessed on 12 October 2020.

Mitra, Annapurna, 2020. *COVID19: A Wake-Up Call for Urban Social Protection in India*. Observer Research Foundation. Retrieved from https://www.orfonline.org /expert-speak/covid19-wake-up-call-urban-social-protection-india-63545/#_ft n6. Accessed on 12 October 2020.

Mitra, Ritwika, 2020. 'Centre to come up with database of tribal migrant workers for livelihood generation amid pandemic', *The New Indian Express*. Retrieved from https://www.newindianexpress.com/nation/2020/jul/09/centre-to-come -up-with-database-of-tribal-migrant-workers-for-livelihood-generation-amid -pandemic-2167473.html. Accessed on 12 October 2020.

Mitra, Rohini, Aarohi Damle and Geetika Varshney, 2020. 'Exclusionary policies push migrants to cities' peripheries', *IndiaSpend*. Retrieved from https://www

.indiaspend.com/exclusionary-policies-push-migrants-to-cities-peripheries/. Accessed on 12 October 2020.

Nandi, Subhalakshmi, 2017. 'Expert's take: Making unpaid work visible creates livelihoods for rural women', *Women*. Retrieved from http://www.unwomen.org /en/news/stories/2017/3/experts-take-subhalakshmi-nandi-unpaid-work#notes. Accessed on 12 October 2020.

Narayana, D., C.S. Venkiteswaran and M.P. Joseph, 2013. *Domestic Migration Labour in Kerala*. Government of Kerala.

Nayyar, Gaurav and Kyoung Yang Kim, 2018. 'India's internal labor migration paradox: The statistical and the real', *World Bank Policy Research Working Paper 8356*. Washington.

Patel, Champa, 2020. *COVID-19: The Hidden Majority in India's Migration Crisis*. Chatham House. Retrieved from https://www.chathamhouse.org/expert/comment /covid-19-hidden-majority-indias-migration-crisis. Accessed on 12 October 2020.

Prabhu, Nagesh, 2020. 'Pandemic will deepen job and livelihood crisis of migrants: Study', *The Hindu*. Retrieved from https://www.thehindu.com/news/national/k arnataka/pandemic-will-deepen-job-and-livelihood-crisis-of-migrants-study/a rticle31439073.ece. Accessed on 12 October 2020.

Press Information Bureau India, 2020. *Union Finance Minister Nirmala Sitharaman Addresses a Press Conference*. Retrieved from https://www.youtube.com/watch? v=hIRebLyGb10. Accessed on 12 October 2020.

Rajan, S.I., 2013. 'Internal migration and youth in India: Main features, trends and emerging challenges', *Discussion Paper*, UNESCO, Delhi.

Rajan, S.I., 2020. 'Kerala's experience with COVID-19: What lessons to learn?', *SocDem Asia Quarterly*, 9(2), 18–22.

Rajan, S.I. and B.D Sami, 2020. 'The way forward on migrant issues', *Frontline*, 22 May.

Rajan, S.I. and P. Sivakumar, 2018. 'Introduction', in S.I. Rajan and P. Sivakumar (Eds.), *Youth Migration in Emerging India: Trends, Challenges and Opportunities*. Delhi: Orient BlackSwan, 1–31.

Rajan, S.I. and M. Sumeetha, 2019. *Handbook on Internal Migration in India*. Delhi: SAGE.

Rajan, S.I. and K.C. Zachariah, 2019. 'Emigration and remittances: New evidence from the Kerala Migration Survey 2018', *Centre for Development Studies (CDS) Working Paper. 483*. Thiruvananthapuram.

Rajan, S.I, Ashwin Kumar and Arokkiaraj Heller, 2019. 'The realities of voting in India: Perspective from internal labour migrants', *Economic and Political Weekly*, LIV(18), 12–14.

Rajan, S.I., P Sivakumar and Aditya Srinivasan, 2020. 'The COVID-19 pandemic and internal labour migration in India: A "Crisis of Mobility"', *Indian Journal of Labour Economics*, 63(4).

Ray, S.S., 2020. 'House panel for expansion of EPF/ESIC net for migrant workers', *Financial Express*. Retrieved from https://www.financialexpress.com/money /house-panel-for-expansion-of-epf-esic-net-for-migrant-workers/2015241/. Accessed on 12 October 2020.

Rukmini, S., 2020. 'How covid-19 locked out women from job', *Livemint*. Retrieved from https://www.livemint.com/news/india/how-covid-19-locked-out-women -from-jobs-11591772350206.html. Accessed on 12 October 2020.

Sapra, Ipsita, 2020. 'Why don't we see the women? The untold story of COVID-19 migration', *Indian Express*. Retrieved from https://indianexpress.com/article /opinion/why-dont-we-see-the-women-the-untold-story-of-covid-19-migration -6378557/. Accessed on 12 October 2020.

Sharan, V P., 2020. 'Jharkhand survey maps skill-sets and find most migrant workers outside central schemes', *The National Herald*. Retrieved from https://www.nat ionalheraldindia.com/india/jharkhand-survey-maps-skill-sets-and-find-most-m igrant-workers-outside-central-schemes. Accessed on 12 October 2020.

Sharma, N.A. and D. Arora, 2011. *Social Protection in India: Issues and Challenges*, Delhi: Institute for Human Development.

Sharma, Palak, 2020. 'Corona and the tragic dynamics of labour economics in India', *The Leaflet*. Retrieved from https://theleaflet.in/corona-and-the-tragic-d ynamics-of-labour-economics-in-india/. Accessed on 12 October 2020.

Simran, Rohini et al., 2019. 'India's social security code, 2019', *The Medium*. Retrieved from https://medium.com/@indiamigration/indias-social-security-co de-2019-4fe5be609faf. Accessed on 12 October 2020.

Srivastava, P., 2020. 'Yogi govt completes skill-mapping of 23.5 lakh migrant workers, 18 lakh want jobs in UP', *Print*. Retrieved from https://theprint.in/ india/yogi-govt-completes-skill-mapping-of-23-5-lakh-migrant-workers-18-lak h-want-jobs-in-up/435450/. Accessed on 12 October 2020.

Srivastava, R., 2013. *A Social Protection Floor for India*, India: International Labour Organization.

Stranded Workers Action Network, 2020. *32 Days and Counting: COVID-19 Lockdown, Migrant Workers, and the Inadequacy of Welfare Measures in India*. Retrieved from https://covid19socialsecurity.files.wordpress.com/2020/05/32 -days-and-counting_swan.pdf. Accessed on 12 October 2020.

The Week, 2020. *Kerala Sets An Example for Rest of India with Its Exceptional Treatment of 'Guest Workers'*. Retrieved from https://www.theweek.in/news/ india/2020/04/20/kerala-sets-an-example-for-rest-of-india-with-its-exceptional -treatment-of-guest-workers.html. Accessed on 12 October 2020.

Tumbe, Chinmoy. 2018. *India Moving: A History of Migration*. Delhi: Penguin.

United Nations Development Programme and Oxford Poverty and Human Development Initiative. 2020. *Charting Pathways out of Multidimensional Poverty: Achieving the SDGs*. New York: United Nations.

Venugopal, Vasudha and Vatsala Gaur, 2020. '3 states finalising databases for benefit of migrant workers', *The Economic Times*. Retrieved from https://ec onomictimes.indiatimes.com/news/politics-and-nation/3-states-finalising-dat abases-for-benefit-of-migrant-workers/articleshow/75983331.cms?from=mdr. Accessed on 12 October 2020.

World Bank, 2020a. 'Employment in services, female (% of female employment) (modeled ILO estimate)'. Retrieved from https://data.worldbank.org/indicator/ SL.SRV.EMPL.FE.ZS?contextual=female-employment-by-sector&view=chart. Accessed on 12 October 2020.

World Bank, 2020b. 'Migration and development brief 32. COVID-19 crisis through a migration lens', *Migration and Development Brief 32*. Washington.

Yadav, Sidharth, 2020. 'Madhya Pradesh launches 'RozgarSetu' scheme for skilled workers', *The Hindu*. Retrieved from https://www.thehindu.com/news/national/other-states/madhya-pradesh-launches-rozgar-setu-scheme-for-skilled-workers/article31701696.ece. Accessed on 12 October 2020.

Zachariah, K.C, E T Mathew and S Irudaya Rajan, 1999. 'Impact of migration on Kerala economy', *CDS Working Paper. 297*. Thiruvananthapuram.

Zachariah, K.C, E T Mathew and S Irudaya Rajan, 2000. 'Socio-economic and demographic consequences of migration in Kerala', *CDS Working Paper. 303*. Thiruvananthapuram.

7 Contestations of citizenship

Migrant labour, a benevolent state, and the COVID-19-induced lockdown in Kerala

Praveena Kodoth

Introduction

The mass exodus of migrant labour in the wake of the national lockdown in March 2020 exposed more than the central government's lack of planning and sensitivity to the conditions of this labour force; it provided a sudden but spontaneous visibility to the full force of the distress and insecurity of migrant workers. To make sense of this harsh reality, it is necessary to go beyond the relationship between this precarious workforce and the nation-state at a time of crisis and to reckon with the more routine failures of citizenship that metamorphosed into a crisis in the first place. The central government was caught off guard by the swiftness with which migrant workers headed back home, indicating a serious lack of awareness and understanding of this workforce.[1] Kerala, however, stood out for the speed with which the government announced a relief package, mobilised volunteers, and instituted measures to mitigate distress with an emphasis on workers who depend on daily earnings and migrant labour. With coordination at various levels of government and communication through the media, the government showed readiness to address gaps in the design and implementation of relief measures. In several migrant hubs, when workers mobilised in public demanding to go back home, government authorities intervened quickly to diffuse protests.

The state government's response to the humanitarian crisis was marked by a rare degree of concern. However, the government employed a rhetoric of care that, along with some hostile public perceptions of migrant workers, brought into view the undermining of the citizenship of migrant workers. The government's insistence on addressing migrant workers as 'guest workers', while suggesting that Kerala as the host state was obliged to provide care steered away, inevitably, from a language of citizenship obligations and rights. Pratap Bhanu Mehta (2020) points out: 'There is something deeply morally odd in using the language of compassion in relation to the state. What we need from the state is not compassion; it is a minimum sense of justice. In fact, the appeals to compassion destructively depoliticise social policy by appealing to sentiment'. Thus, the depiction of protests by migrant workers in everyday conversations as 'ingratitude' fitted well within the state's approach.

Migrant labourers are considered indispensable to Kerala's economy. If their exodus forced them into full public view across the country, they were already visible in Kerala, i.e., there was recognition of their presence, albeit in specific forms. A form of state-conferred visibility in the form of pioneering welfare schemes offered migrant workers the possibility of at least minimal social protection.[2] But migrant workers laid claim to a more contentious form of visibility. For instance, they have sought to mark their identity and achieve solidarity by coming together in public places like a Sunday market in Perambavoor, a large migrant hub near Ernakulum, and by engaging sporadically in protests (Prasad, M., 2016). Migrant hubs have theatres screening Hindi, Odiya, and Bengali films and churches that hold mass for migrant workers in their languages (Sudhir, 2016), which also merit study as distinctive spaces for marking identity. The state-society complex in Kerala, which includes the police and other government agencies, mainstream trade unions and the Malayali public have been implicated in curtailing freedoms of expression, assembly, and association of migrant workers. For instance, Prasad Aleyamma (2017) points out with reference to Perambavoor that migrant workers are produced as a threat to public order, which serves to legitimise police harassment and to justify demands for surveillance.

I examine contestations of citizenship of migrant workers in Kerala during and before the lockdown as have been apparent in the stoking of suspicion and fear against them in the context of protests or when a crime is committed in a migrant hub. As public perceptions, police actions, and underlying social relations produce migrant workers as 'outsiders' and expose the fault lines of a benevolent state, I argue that state-conferred visibility in the form of welfare does not guarantee enfranchised citizenship. The undermining of migrant citizenship becomes even more apparent in contrast to Non Resident Keralites (NRKs) who are an important political constituency and are appealed to by the state in a language that grants them a position of privilege and power.

Migrant labour and the lockdown response in Kerala

A widely cited estimate derived from a study by the Gulati Institute of Finance and Taxation in 2013 puts the current number of inter-state migrant workers at more than 3.5 million.[3] The major source states, West Bengal, Bihar, Assam, and Uttar Pradesh, accounted for about 70 per cent of migrants, with each of them contributing between 20 and 15 per cent. However, only 5.09 lakh migrant workers are registered under the Awas scheme (see note 2), a health insurance scheme administered by the labour department and a survey by the labour department during the lockdown enumerated a little over 4.34 lakh migrant workers in camps in the state. This may be only a fraction of migrant workers in the state. Problems of estimation of migrant workers, encountered nation-wide, are intertwined with the failure of governments to design and implement social protection (Samaddar, 2020b).

It is obvious that Kerala had better outreach and documentation of camps compared to other states. The first report submitted to the Supreme Court on 31 March 2020 in response to a PIL showed that Kerala accounted for 65 per cent of migrant shelter camps (18,912 migrant camps) and housed nearly 50 per cent of migrants (over 3 lakhs) documented across the country (Writ petition (Civil) No 468/2020). Considering Kerala's small population share and that it accounts for only a very small share of all migrant labour in the country, these are disproportionately large figures.

The state labour commissioner, who has received praise for his proactive responses, observed that 'the idea of camp was conceptual, rather than in physical terms' (G Plus news, 2020). The reference here is to the distribution of migrant labour in shelter camps arranged by the state government, employer-provided camps, and the difficult-to-enumerate rented accommodations across the state. However, it elides over the possibility that a large section of migrant labour were not enumerated. Nevertheless, official categorisation according to the nature of employment and residence streamlined planning. Decentralised executions of plans meant that there were variations according to districts, but it was apparent that workers in shelters were relatively well taken care of compared to workers whose contractors/employers were expected to provide for their food and other basic needs (Arnimesh, 2020). Migrant protests were fuelled at least partly by the dearth of essential provisions among those who resided in rented accommodation (*The Hindu*, 29 March).

Reports indicate that officials acted on specific complaints when employers/contractors failed to make provision for food and water for workers. But in some instances, repeated appeals were made and higher-level officials responded with alacrity where local officials had failed. The SWAN report noted that cases reported from Kerala were resolved with help from the local administration, but in one instance no action was taken even after follow-up. 'The workers also said that they were reluctant to call the control room as they were afraid of being harassed. The SWAN volunteers interceded with the District Collectorate and the matter was sorted out'.[4]

The labour commissioner's direct intervention enabled migrant workers from Kalahandi in Odisha who were detained by their employer to return home and ensured that the workers were paid their wages which their employer had held back (Jena, 2020), a tactic that is used by employers in the state to prevent workers from leaving. When it was reported that plantation owners and managers in Idukki were not able to provide food for migrant labour, the state government, based on investigation of a report from the Idukki district labour officer, gave instructions that migrant workers employed on plantations in Idukki district and not in possession of ration cards should be provided free rations that would be financed from the CMDRF/SDRF (G O no. 113/2020, Public Distribution Division).

Interventions by the state government underlined carefully devised strategies to prevent unrest. Measures were taken to reach out to migrant workers in their own languages through call centres and pamphlets, to ensure that they were able to communicate with their families back home, provision was made for monitoring of health, counselling services were set up, and even recreation facilities were provided in shelters. Recognising that the distress of migrant workers went beyond essential provisions, the state government was among the first to appeal to the Centre to run trains for them to return homes if they so desired. By June, nearly 58 per cent or 252,444 migrant workers enumerated in camps had left the state in 180 special trains from across the state (Sai Kiran, 2020). The measures taken by the state government during the lockdown were consistent with a pre-existing welfare approach but they must be seen alongside expressions of hostility and xenophobia against migrant workers (discussed in the following section).

Inter-state migrant workers and citizenship in Kerala

Explaining Kerala's performance in keeping the infection and death rates low in the first few months of the pandemic, Patrick Heller (2020) underscored the 'robust nature of Kerala's social compact' and likened the pandemic to a 'physical exam of the social body' that put public trust to its biggest ever test. However, if public trust has defined the state's ability in Kerala to 'elicit compliance' (a reference to the willingness of citizens to comply with the measures taken by the state), we also need to be attentive of the fractures in the social body in Kerala. With the rapidly increasing numbers of migrant workers in Kerala and as a section of them reside with their families, educate their children, and develop stronger stakes in local society, the social body in Kerala is clearly becoming more diverse. This reality pushes against the problems with an approach that evades the question of political rights.

A case in point is the use of the term 'guest workers', which was meant to convey a caring approach. However, as migration scholar, Binoy Peter was quick to point out, by using the term, the 'government seems to be reminding them to leave after their work is finished, which is discriminatory. They have the right to be here' (cited in Paliath, 2020). The term is reminiscent of the guest worker programme in postwar Germany, which politely spelt out temporality in residence and the Kafala (guest) system in the Middle East that gives impunity to the police and nationals to discipline the immigrant workforce (Kodoth, 2020).

This is not merely an issue of nomenclature. In response to allegations of illegal migration and criminal activity, successive governments in Kerala have sought to increase bureaucratic controls over migrant workers. At one point, migrant workers were required to obtain police clearance cards that vouched for their credentials – their place of birth and lack of criminal antecedents (Prasad, 2017). Such mechanisms of control also recall immigration regimes for as Caroline Vandenabeele points out: 'Legal identity, or the right to be recognized by the government of the country of which one is a citizen, is a primary right that exists regardless of whether one has a document to prove this citizenship ... [O]fficial, government-issued and -recognized documents ... do not *confer* legal identity; they merely *confirm* it' (cited in Bhabha, 2011: 5).

Ironically, in Kerala, where workers' protests are staple fare, protests by migrant workers during the lockdown were used to stoke suspicion and fear. A sample of messages circulated on social media read: 'Migrant labourers from West Bengal, Assam, Bihar and UP could take control over Perambavoor town in less than 10 minutes. They will not allow us to flee. Our situation would become worse than that of Pandits, who fled Kashmir valley' (Ameerudhin, 2020).

The idea that migrant workers pose a threat to the territorial sovereignty of the Malayali people raises fundamental contestation of migrant citizenship. This notion of sovereignty is not threatened, however, by existing state-conferred visibility. A recent expression of state-conferred visibility in the form of the celebration of the achievements of the daughter of a migrant worker from Bihar is instructive. On 23 August 2020, Payal Kumari made headlines when she secured the first rank in the final examination of the history and archaeology course at the MG University in Kottayam.[5] She was feted by the chief minister: 'What makes her success special is the fact that her parents are guest workers' (cited in Phillip, 2020). Interviewed widely, she was quoted as saying that her success belonged to Kerala and that she could not have made this kind of progress had her family remained in her home state (Kuriakose, 2020). As the media recounted the many acts of kindness from her teachers and school and college authorities that enabled her and her family to overcome seemingly unsurmountable odds, it was difficult to miss how the girl's achievements were presented as seamless with those of a socially progressive and caring state and a generous society.

Contrast this with the responsibility for crime committed by migrant workers which is systematically displaced on to the social body of migrants. A slew of allegations, mostly unsubstantiated, are levelled against migrant workers, suggesting that they are a threat to public order and public health as they engage in criminal activities, alcohol, and substance abuse, lack basic hygiene, and offer a safe haven for law breakers, terrorists, and illegal migrants. A reporter pointed out:

> The locals, including the contractors, plot a direct correlation between the unhygienic circumstances in which they live and their 'criminal tendencies'. 'They don't care about anything else but money. They want to come to Kerala, live in the dirtiest of ways, commit a burglary and then leave', says Joseph Babu, a contractor.
>
> (Thomas, 2013)

The contention that the problem lies with migrant workers diverts attention from state practices, policies, and social relations. Pointing out that it is the government and not migrant workers who are responsible for addressing problems of cleanliness and illegal activity, an activist described that it is the living conditions of migrant workers that foster ill health:

> There is scarcity of clean water. They [migrant workers] do not have adequate toilet facilities. Ten to 20 people live in small huts. They are anonymous and there are no records. There is no system to provide vaccinations or other forms of necessary medical care to them.
>
> (TB Mini cited in Shaheena, 2016)

The rape and murder of a young law student in 2016, which was eventually traced to a migrant worker, was a defining moment in mobilising legitimacy for surveillance of migrant workers. Multiple forms of marginality intersected in representations of the victim and the suspect. In the immediate aftermath of the crime, the media treated the victim, a Dalit from a poor family, with insensitively revealing her name and questioning her academic credentials before catapulting her into the position of 'Kerala's daughter' even as it generated paranoia about migrant labour (Zacharias, 2016).

Amidst growing tensions, a mob lynched a migrant worker who arrived in the state soon after the incident, reportedly on the suspicion that he was a thief. Bobby Thomas, a migrant rights activist pointed out:

This is only a symptom of the abhorrence and intolerance that Malayalee society displays towards migrant workers. Now public demands for registering them with the police are on the rise … Why police? The government has other mechanisms to keep a record of migrants coming to Kerala. Even local self-governments can play a role.

(Cited in Shaheena 2016)

The question exposes the failures of a benevolent state in protecting the rights of migrant workers in Kerala. Notably, fear of the police can prevent migrants from speaking openly. As 'the already existing xenophobia has increased', migrant workers were reluctant to speak of police interrogation or even their living or working conditions (Thomas cited in Shaheena, 2016).

But displacing the responsibility for crime on to migrant labour also diverts attention more specifically from the state's responsibility to ensure women's safety. A migrant activist is forced to state the obvious – that the problem of gender-based crime is not confined to migrant labour:

Instead of keeping the migrants under the scanner each time a rape is committed, Kerala's government and society must find ways to make the state a safer place for women to live in. The statistics being bandied about in the media amount to this: In 2015, every 43 minutes saw a new crime against a woman in the state. And, on average, a woman was raped almost every six hours. Few migrants, if any, have anything to do with this astounding crime rate.

(Fr PA Chacko, cited in Prasad, S. 2016)

An environment of suspicion that is generated in the wake of crime has served to remind migrant workers of their 'outsider' status. The rape and murder of a woman in Perambavoor in 2019 'brought back that by-now familiar sense of alienation that visits the likes of Rajendar [a migrant worker] every time a migrant is hauled up by police' (Praveen, 2019). Rajendar, who has spent the past two decades in Kerala, arriving in the state at the age of 16, told the reporter that people 'need to realise that every land has its share of good and bad people, and there is no place full of good people alone'. He lives in Perambavoor with his family in circumstances that could not be very different from those of Payal Kumari, whose academic achievement was celebrated. Both spoke fluently in Malayalam and their families worked hard to make a living in Kerala. Payal Kumari was quoted as saying that she felt so safe in Kerala that she could walk on the streets at night without causing concern to her parents and that she was never made to feel like an outsider (Kuriakose, 2020). While this may suggest a certain fluidity and layering in the experiences of migrants, the association of criminality with migrant workers exposes a bed rock of congealed hostility.

In contrast to individual achievements of migrants, whether in education, sports, or art, the marking of identity and difference are political acts that may be perceived as threats to sovereignty. What emerges from the above analysis is a binary view of migrant labour as a threat to public order who must therefore submit to state surveillance or quintessentially apolitical actors, whose achievements showcase the progressive credentials of the state. It is instructive, in this light, that the state sees welfare and surveillance as inextricably bound together. Epitomising this is the Awas scheme (see note 2), which was launched in the aftermath of the 2016 rape and murder case that exposed migrants to heightened suspicion. The objectives of the scheme were 'to ensure collection of information about inter-state migrant workers in Kerala and to provide health security'. Information referred to bio metrics and personal data of migrant workers (GO (Ordinary) no. 1365/2016, Department of Labour and Skills).

Crucially, the problem of migrant citizenship cannot be seen in isolation from the larger question of labour rights in Kerala. Routine forms of discrimination against migrant labour are evident in comparatively low wages (than that of local labour) and poor working and living conditions. Migrant labour is excluded from the significant gains made by local labour in both the formal and informal sectors. Mainstream trade unions are embedded in local structures of power and have colluded with big business interests to undermine the bargaining power of migrant workers (Prasad-Aleyamma, 2017). In this context, Prasad, M (2016) notes that migrant workers have sought to claim citizenship by forging alliances with their employers in the face of collusion by mainstream trade unions with the state and big businesses interests.

The All India Trade Union Congress, affiliated to the Communist Party of India, formed a separate Migrant Workers Union in 2013 but efforts to organise migrant workers are stymied by the conventional approach of organising designed for factory labour. The first state conference of the Kerala Migrant Workers' Union in 2017 acknowledged that rights achieved by local labour 'a long time ago' were not extended to migrant workers, who suffered from non-payment of minimum wages; exploitation by contractors; lack of proper living space; and proper service conditions, including health and shelter (*The Hindu*, 2 April 2017).

Interestingly, trade unions and the police fail to see that mobility is a condition that demands fundamental reworking of social and political institutions. The present structure of trade unions is too rigid to accommodate migrant labour except in separate unions that undermine labour solidarity. Being unconventional, the Self Employed Women's Association may offer a model as it registers membership in an umbrella organisation, irrespective of the place of work and occupation of the worker. Another way is to think in terms of portability of membership from place to place and even occupation to occupation given the nature of the times where necessary skill sets are subject to rapid change.

Expatriate Malayali labour

An estimated 3.0 million Keralites work in the Middle East. Of the approximately 3 lakh NRKs who had returned from COVID-19 hit countries by mid-April 2020, 1.65 lakh had lost their jobs (Kuttappan, 2020). The relations of the state with inter-state migrant workers, on the one hand, and NRKs, on the other, provide some instructive insights. The state appeals to NRKs in a language of merit that grants them a position of power and privilege. During the lockdown, for instance, the need to facilitate their return home was justified repeatedly with reference to their economic contributions or what the state owes to them as 'gratitude'. Also the two major political blocs in the state, the United Democratic Front and the Left Democratic Front, compete to be seen as the protectors of NRK interests. During the lockdown, the opposition accused the government of not being in earnest about facilitating the return of NRKs. A government order refusing to provide free quarantine for returning expatriates which said that *Pravasis* and 'guest workers' could not be treated as equal became hugely controversial, notwithstanding the substantially different costs that would be involved.

The efforts to woo NRKs are evidence of their collective power. Unlike in the case of inter-state migrant labour, state-conferred visibility of NRKs coincides substantially with visibility carved out by NRKs. Kerala is a pioneer in establishing a separate government department (Non Resident Keralites Association – NORKA) to serve the interests of NRKs. NORKA offers several welfare schemes for NRKs and returnee workers and has been organising the *Loka Kerala Sabha*, an occasion that like the *Pravasi Divas* celebrates expatriate achievements. During the lockdown, the government announced the Dream Kerala Project to tap the skills and experience of return migrants and also distributed Rs. 5,000 each to over 20,000 NRKs who were prevented from returning to the jobs. Going beyond welfare to a measure of political voice, representatives of NRKs are on the board of NORKA, whereas inter-state migrant workers are not involved in the design and governance of welfare schemes. NRKs also have their own associations to intervene in matters concerning them and to lobby with the government.

However, NRKs are not one homogeneous bloc. The celebration of the achievements of NRKs invariably excludes migrant domestic workers

(MDW), comprising women mostly from economically distressed families who are possibly the single largest occupational group of women migrants from the state. There is little recognition of their substantial contribution to the betterment of some of the most socially marginal households in the state, those of widows and separated women (Kodoth, 2020). A discourse of merit that defines the government's response to male migrant workers and more affluent migrants has deleterious implications for groups that are not seen as worthy of celebration.

The visibility of MDWs in Kerala is defined usually by narratives of abuse and harassment, but these narratives have fallen strangely silent since the pandemic hit. Reports from the Middle East suggest that MDWs may be subject to increased workloads, paid lower salaries, at greater risk of contracting COVID because their jobs involve tasks of cleaning and close proximity with employers (Aoun, 2020). The Indian government outreach to domestic workers is usually poor and during the crisis there have been no specific measures to protect them. Many MDWs defy unjust state regulation, which restrict their right to mobility, and migrate to the Middle East through irregular channels. The government's approach to MDWs exposes the intersecting gender, class, and caste divide within Kerala and undermines citizenship (Kodoth, 2020).

Conclusion: Search for justice-based solidarity

Inter-state migrant labour in Kerala was granted a form of visibility through at least minimal social protection prior to and during the lockdown. At the same time, state practices and social relations have been implicated in producing them as 'outsiders' and denying them political rights. Thus, I have argued that state-conferred visibility has not guaranteed enfranchised citizenship. The analysis in the chapter presents two kinds of contrasts that underscore the failures of citizenship of inter-state migrant workers in Kerala and expose the faultlines of a benevolent state. While the extension of welfare to migrant workers and the celebration of their individual achievements are presented as seamless with a socially progressive and caring state and society, migrant protests are represented as a threat to sovereignty and the responsibility for crime committed by migrant workers is displaced *en masse* on to migrant labour. The second contrast is in the position of NRKs and inter-state migrant labour. Whereas the state appeals to NRKs in a language that grants them a position of privilege and power and state-conferred visibility coincides substantially with visibility sought by NRKs, the rhetoric of benevolence used to appeal to inter-state migrant workers and the discordance between state-conferred visibility and visibility staked by migrant workers underscore the failure of a benevolent state.

However, NRKs are differentiated and among them MDWs are not seen as meritorious which indicates some similarities between the position of MDWs and that of inter-state migrant workers.

Mehta (2020) has pointed out that 'genuine solidarity, that speaks the language of justice, will ask hard questions about rights, institutional obligations, processes and accountability'. Labour rights are crucial to the issue of justice-based solidarity for migrant workers. At present, inter-state migrant labour is excluded from the substantial gains made by local labour in Kerala and has an uneasy relationship with the mainstream trade unions. Going further, as Samaddar (2020b: 39) observes the struggle for justice calls for the recognition of the vulnerabilities and struggles of people, which mandate a caring model of power that is socially regenerative, enriching of life, and produces solidarity. He argues that workplace rights and social protection are inadequate as migrant workers are invisible in politics (p 33). Indeed, in Kerala the spatial clustering of migrants could favour the emergence of migrant workers as elected representatives at the local level. The fear of and push back against migrant efforts to register their political existence and the binding of social protection to bureaucratic controls may be seen in this light.

Notes

1 Samaddar (2020a) points out that the exodus demonstrated the conditions in the informal economy and the near absence of social protection which fosters the circulation of workers between their villages and the cities, giving migrant workers little reason to remain in the destination and many reasons to leave.

2 The Kerala Migrant Workers Welfare Scheme, 2010, the first of its kind in the country, to provide accident/medical care for up to Rs. 25,000; Rs. 1 lakh to the family in case of death; children's education allowance; and termination benefits of Rs. 25,000 after five years of work to registered migrants. Awas offers registered workers free treatment of up to Rs. 25,000 from government empanelled hospitals and if a worker dies, the family receives Rs. 2 lakh as compensation. There is also the Roshini project aimed at inclusion of migrant children in schools and Changathi, a Malayalam literacy initiative for migrant workers.

3 The study estimated that there were about 2.5 million inter-state migrant workers in Kerala in 2013 and that the numbers could be expected to increase by about 2.35 lakh every year based on data on mobility from the railways (Narayana and Venkiteswaran, 2013).

4 SWAN (2020). For a discussion of gaps in implementation and responsiveness of higher-level state authorities, see also Roy (2020: 78).

5 Earlier in the year, a migrant woman from Bihar was similarly feted when she topped the Malayalam literacy exam with full marks (*The Hindu*, February 16, 2020). There are other examples as well such as an exhibition of paintings by a migrant worker from Bengal in Kozhikode (Shaheena, 2016).

References

Ameerudhin, T.A., 2020. 'Vilification campaign mounts against migrant labourers in Kerala post lockdown protests', April 10. Retrieved from https://www.onm anorama.com/news/kerala/2020/04/10/villification-campaign-against-migrant -workers-in-kerala-after-lockdown-protests.html. Accessed on 15 October 2020.

Aoun, Rana, 2020. 'COVID-19 impact on female migrant domestic workers in the middle east', *GBV AOR Helpdesk*. Retrieved from https://gbvaor.net/sites/default/files/2020-05/COVID-19%20and%20Impact%20on%20Vulnerable%2 0Female%20Migrant%20Domestic%20Workers%5B5%5D.pdf. Accessed on 15 October 2020.

Arnimesh, Shanker, 2020. 'Rotis, mobile recharges, carrom boards — how Kerala fixed its migrant worker anger', *Print*, 18 April. Retrieved from https://theprin t.in/india/rotis-mobile-recharges-carrom-boards-how-kerala-fixed-its-migrant -worker-anger/403937/. Accessed on 15 October 2020.

Bhabha, J., 2011. 'Introduction', in J. Bhabha, ed., *Children Without a State: A Human Rights Challenge*, MIT Press: Cambridge, MA.

G.O. (Ordinary) no 1325/2016/labour, Government of Kerala, Department of Labour and Skills, dated 20/10/16.

G O no. 113/2020, Government of Kerala, Public distribution division, dated April 24.

G Plus News, 2020. 'SRC, India conducted webinar on 'COVID-19 and the handling of migrants: Kerala experiences', *G Plus News*, 07 July.

Heller, Patrick, 2020. 'A virus, social democracy, and dividends for Kerala', *The Hindu*, 18 April.

Jena, Sujata, 2020. 'A good samaritan labour commissioner of Kerala and light at the end of a tunnel for Odisha guest workers', *Countercurrents.org*, 22 June.

Kodoth, Praveena, 2020. 'In the shadow of the state: Recruitment and migration of women as domestic workers to the middle east', *Background Paper*, International Labour Organisation, July.

Kuriakose, Ronnie, 2020. '"My success belongs to Kerala": Migrant worker's daughter on securing first rank in MG varsity exam', *Onmanorama*, 26 August. Retrieved from https://www.onmanorama.com/news/kerala/2020/08/26/payal -kumari-migrant-workers-daughter-secures-first-rank.html. Accessed on 15 October 2020.

Kuttappan, Rejimon, 2020. '1.65 lakh Keralites returned from COVID-Hit countries due to job loss', 20 August. Retrieved from https://www.thelede.in/inclusion/20 20/08/20/165-lakh-keralites-returned-from-covid-hit-countries-due-to-job-loss. Accessed on 15 October 2020.

Mehta, Pratap Bhanu, 2020. 'Beyond solidarity: The migrant labour and the unemployed will be demanding their rights, not our mercy', *Indian Express*, 18 April. Retrieved from https://indianexpress.com/article/opinion/columns/coron avirus-covid-19-india-lockdown-migrant-labourers-6367384/. Accessed on 15 October 2020.

Narayana, D and C. S. Venkiteswaran, 2013. *Domestic Migrant Labour in Kerala*, GIFT, Thiruvananthapuram.

Paliath, Shreehari, 2020. 'Now is the time to show India cares about its migrants', Interview with Binoy Peter, *Indiaspend.com*, 15 April. Retrieved from https://www.indiaspend.com/now-is-the-time-to-show-india-cares-about-its-migrants/. Accessed on 15 October 2020.

Phillip, Shaju, 2020. 'In Kerala, migrant's daughter tops BA exam, earns CM's praise', *Indian Express*, 24 August.

Prasad, M., 2016. 'Migration and production of space: Labour, capital and the state in Kerala, India', Unpublished PhD thesis, Jawaharlal Nehru University, New Delhi.

Prasad, Srinivasa, 2016. 'Jisha rape and murder: Kerala must stop looking at all migrant workers with suspicion', *FirstPost*, 07 May. Retrieved from https://www.firstpost.com/india/jisha-kerala-migrant-workers-gulf-nations-rape-crime-against-women-2769080.html. Accessed on 15 October 2020.

Prasad-Aleyamma, Mythri, 2017. 'Cards and carriers: Migration, identification and surveillance in Kerala, South India', *Contemporary South Asia*, doi:10.1080/09584935.2017.1407293.

Praveen, M. P., 2019. 'Migrants rue being stamped as criminals', *The Hindu*, Kochi, 29 November.

PTI, 2020. 'Bihari migrant woman emerges topper in Malayalam literacy exam', *The Hindu*, 16 February.

Roy, Rajat, 2020. 'The sudden visibility of Sangram Tudu', in R. Samaddar, ed. *Borders of an Epidemic in Borders of an Epidemic: COVID 19 and Migrant Labour*, Calcutta Research Group, Kolkata pp 76–82.

Saikiran, KP., 2020. '58% of migrant workers go back, Kerala to feel pinch', *Times of India*, 12 June.

Samaddar, Ranabir, 2020a. *Introduction: Borders of an Epidemic in Borders of an Epidemic: COVID 19 and Migrant Labour*, Calcutta Research Group, Kolkata, pp. 1–23.

Samaddar, Ranabir, 2020b. *Burdens of an Epidemic: A Policy Perspective on COVID 19 and Migrant Labour*, Calcutta Research Group, Kolkata.

Shaheena, K.K., 2016. 'Migrant workers in Kerala: The stigma', *Open the Magazine*, 14 July. Retrieved from https://openthemagazine.com/features/india/migrant-workers-in-kerala-the-stigma/. Accessed on 15 October 2020.

Sudhir, T.S. 2016. 'In wake of dalit law student's rape, Kerala debates demand for a database of migrants', *Scroll.in*, 21 June. Retrieved from https://scroll.in/article/810312/in-wake-of-dalit-law-students-rape-kerala-debates-demand-for-a-database-of-migrants. Accessed on 15 October 2020.

SWAN, 2020. '32 days and counting: COVID lockdown, migrant workers and the inadequacy of welfare measures in India', *Stranded Workers Action Network*, 1 May

Thomas, Suresh P., 2013. 'Fear and loathing in Kerala', *fountainink.in*, 04 Feb. Retrieved from https://fountainink.in/reportage/fear-and-loathing-in-kerala. Accessed on 15 October 2020.

Writ petition (Civil), 468/2020 in Supreme Court of India in the case Shri Alakh Alok Srivastava Vs Union of India.

Zacharias, Prabha, 2016. 'Perumbavoor rape shows why it's time Kerala did a self check about progressiveness', *Indian Express*, 13 May.

8 Protecting livelihood, health, and decency of work

Paid domestic workers in times of COVID-19

S. Anandhi and E. Deepa

Introduction

The COVID-19 virus, combined with the state measures to contain it through lockdowns, has severely affected one of Chennai's indomitable informal workforces, the paid domestic workers. In the last three decades, Chennai has seen a phenomenal growth of paid domestic work along with the growth of other service sectors. A large section of poor women who live in the slums of the city have taken up paid domestic work as viable employment for their family's survival. There are roughly about 1.8 million poor women in Tamil Nadu who work as paid domestic workers. Their work is primarily a dually informalised work since it is performed in the private informal sphere of the domestic with women who are often invisible as 'workers' in addition to the work being contractual with no employment protection or worker benefits such as the provident fund, health insurance, accident benefits, or old age pension. For example, the paid domestic workers are not covered by the Workmen's Compensation Act as they are not treated as 'workman' by a narrow definition given in this conservative act[1] that excludes any employment of 'casual nature' or the ones that are not seen as involving 'trade' or 'business'. The paid domestic work is also excluded from a range of worker's protective and welfare acts such as the Minimum Wages Act 1948, Maternity Benefit Act 1961, and the Contract Labour (regulation and Abolition) Act 1970;[2] therefore, they are not entitled to even minimum worker's benefits such as weekly holidays, sick leave, and maternity leave. There is also a problem of fixing the categories of domestic work as skilled and unskilled, with most works being categorised as unskilled, leading to low pay for these workers. For example, in a recent minimum wage notification even cooking, child care, and elderly care have been categorised as unskilled work, leading to low pay for such arduous care work (Sarkar, 2019). The minimum wage fixed by the state of Tamil Nadu for these workers is woefully inadequate, which has not taken into account the specific nature of vulnerabilities and the intense physical labour involved in this work.[3] Working as part-time or full time and as live-in for 8–10 hours a day either in one house or in multiple houses these workers are subjected to various forms of gendered exploitations, sexual harassment at the workplace, for instance. Further, with their labour being expropriated without adequate compensations or any work security, the livelihood of the domestic workers is extremely fragile and uncertain.

With the pandemic, paid domestic workers are facing the crisis of employment and nonpayment of salary, in addition to the pre-existing social stigmas against them. Some of them are forced to go for work amidst the virus crisis, risking their life with no health security. A large contingent of these women workers belongs to the slums of Chennai with inadequate housing and sanitation facilities and with lack of income to meet any health crisis. Under these abject living conditions, they also share the undue burden of the social distancing policy of the state. Keeping in mind the many woes and challenges faced by the domestic workers during the pandemic, in this chapter, we suggest various measures for social and health protection of these workers along with other labour welfare measures that are on records for many decades without being strictly implemented.

Challenges faced by the paid domestic workers in the context of COVID-19

Crisis of employment

The impact of COVID-19 on women domestic workers is profound and sometimes immeasurable. The first major problem faced by these workers is sudden unemployment, which is no less a threat to their lives than the virus itself. In compliance with the lockdown, many employers have requested their domestic workers not to come for work until they are called back (ILO News, 7 May 2020). This has created enormous uncertainty for the paid domestic workers who have begun to fear job loss. A domestic worker from north Chennai, in her interview with us, captured this anxiety thus: 'If I stay at home without work my family will starve, if I leave home defying the lockdown, corona will get me. I dread to think but dared to go for work [*uyirai panayam vechuthan velaikku pogiren*]'.[4] Though at present we do not have adequate data on the extent of job loss among the paid domestic workers,[5] the recent protest by the domestic workers belonging to Pen Thozholalar Sangam (Women Workers' Association) and their demand that the state immediately issue an order to the employers to take back the domestic workers make clear that the crisis of job loss is real, intense, and that it has severely affected the livelihood of these workers (*The Newsminute*, 2 September 2020).

Some employers have shrewdly dismissed these workers just before the lockdown and promised to take them back once the lockdown is eased. However, some of these workers are not convinced about getting their jobs back. After 21 days of lockdown, a worker in her interview said that much of her trepidation is about her employers, who might get used to doing their housework by themselves and not call her back and that as they too would get only half pay, they would not pay her salary during the lockdown. 'I am not sure if they will call me back for work [*yenna velaikku vetchipaangalaanu theriyala*]' was her remark on the plight of unemployment. Several domestic workers in Chennai city have not received their monthly wages for the past two months. Some of them have received only half pay for the month of March and nothing for the following months (Ramakrishnan, 2020). A woman who works for bachelors said her employers paid only half the salary for three months and were also demanding her to be present for work when she faced the problem of transport. According to her, they were also unwilling to advance loan for any health contingency. Some workers have risked police vigilance and, putting their own health at risk, have gone to work so that they do not lose the job. They also undertook more work in these households where the demands of care work as well as sanitation work have increased due to the COVID-19 crisis.

Reverse migration of families in search of rural livelihood have forced some of these domestic workers to leave Chennai without a hope of getting back to their work in the city. Our prediction is that due to job loss in other sectors of informal work, with no employment guarantee scheme for urban workers, there could be a huge supply of domestic workers from poor women seeking job for survival. This would not only increase the competition among the workers but also reduce their bargaining capacity in terms of wages and other benefits, including their capacity to negotiate their demands for toilet facilities within employer's home or for any other health security.

Low pay, liquidity crunch, and welfare crisis

A large proportion of women domestic workers are middle-aged married women, among whom a substantial number are widows or divorced or living with alcoholic, abusive husbands with financial instability in the family. We may note that men in these families too lack any stable income and most of them are casual workers who work in the informal sector as construction workers, sanitary workers, and so on, or are self-employed as auto drivers, electricians, plumbers, painters, etc. They too have lost their income due to the lockdown, thus multiplying the family's hardship. With a monthly income, these women workers are often the main providers for their family and therefore are encountering the worst situation of liquidity crunch in their homes at a time when the cost of essential commodities has gone up and their familiar neighbourhood stores where they have monthly accounts or loans to purchase household items are shut for a while. Some of them told us they could not venture out to borrow money from their employers who could also not transfer the same through phone banking since many of these workers were not familiar with such technologies. The divorced or separated women workers often do not hold ration cards or bank accounts to avail the government welfare schemes during the pandemic.

Pressure to pay rent on time despite the Tamil Nadu Government order (G.O. no.195, 30 March 2020) not to collect rent for these two months has forced many of them to borrow money for high interest. One single woman worker narrated her experience of being harassed by her landlord thus: 'I am living in a hut paying Rs. 2,500 per month as rent. The owner has been harassing me to pay the rent and I had to fight with him two days reminding him of the Government order not to force collect rent. Finally he relented but it is still like a dagger on my neck'. The state welfare provisions, as many pointed out, are not adequate to meet the needs of the entire family.[6]

Though Tamil Nadu Domestic Welfare Board has been allocated special relief funds to manage the crisis of the workers during the pandemic, the Board suffers from long years of inactivity with no proper registration of the domestic workers to deliver the welfare schemes. It is estimated that the Greater Chennai alone would have 5.5 lakh domestic workers, whereas by 2009, only 64,825 women workers were registered with the Board. Among the registered, only 17,066 members have received any benefits from the Welfare Board and many of them are not even aware of manual workers' welfare schemes.

Return to work: New woes

In Chennai, ever since the slums have been relocated in faraway Kannagi Nagar and Perumpakkam, the paid domestic workers living in these resettlement colonies travel a long way to the central parts of the city for work, spending a huge amount as transport cost. One may note here that in the case of domestic work, trust, loyalty to employers, and regularity bring the workers several benefits. Therefore, women workers endure long-distance travel to keep their relationship and work intact. In order to retain their work with their previous employers, these workers shell out a huge amount of their salary as travel cost (Coelho et al., 2013). With the easing of the lockdown when these workers were expected to return to work, many of them could not do so since their mobility was severely hampered by the lack of transport facilities. The anxiety of losing work due to the lack of transport was expressed thus by a young worker who lives in Perumpakkam and works in Mylapore: 'I do not know what to do. If I do not take up the work when called, the employers might go for other workers and I stand to lose these houses of work. I cannot walk such a long distance for work; I am in a fix and caught in a dilemma [*En nilamai, iruthalai kolli erumbu madhiri*]'.

Care workers or carriers of virus?

'Will we come to work with the virus when we care for them? [*avangala paathukira nanga noiyoda velaikku varuvoma?*]', asked a worker during our interview with her. With the spread of virus, the stigma attached to the domestic work and the workers are reinforced through means of identifying these workers as carriers of virus (Viswanath, 2020). In Chennai, taking into consideration the upper-caste class anxiety about manual workers as being the carriers of any disease, many resident associations have barred entry of domestic workers and drivers into their premises. This is despite the state relaxation of lockdown rules (DT Next, 10 June 2020). Karpagam, a worker from the Pen Thozhilar Sangam, noted that the 'members of Residents' Welfare Associations (RWAs) of various apartments have told them not to visit the apartment for work until next year'. She further observed that the affluent apartment dwellers 'are not ready to take workers who hail from homes in the Tamil Nadu Slum Clearance Board' (*The Newsminute*, 2 September 2020). Similarly, A. Kumari, who works for several houses in an apartment complex, said that she was asked to leave immediately once the employers got to know that she lives in the Tamil Nadu Slum Clearance Board tenements in Perumbakkam (*The Hindu*, 3 September 2020). 'It has been three months and I am struggling to find a job', she said. In cases where they have been called back to work, severe restrictions and surveillance are put in place to the extent of denying the dignity of the workers. One worker confided that after the lockdown, new kinds of surveillance practices are put in place in her employer's house, making her feel uneasy and self-conscious about her hygiene status. 'Interrogating me as to whether I keep my house clean and whether everyone at home bathed, etc., in addition to the routine wash of my feet with turmeric water before entering their house have become a new routine making me feel conscious of my working class status'. Another worker felt that though maintaining hygiene and self-distancing are good to keep the virus away it should not be used to stigmatise or cast aspersions on the workers. In some residential apartments domestic workers are prohibited from using the lift to reach houses in several floors. So far it appears that instructions on maintaining social distancing given to these workers is used in subtle ways to reinforce the pre-existing stigmas against the workers who seem to risk their own life for want of adequate provisions for hand-washing, self-isolation, and wearing of masks or any other personal protective gears.

Paid domestic workers and the unpaid care work

The COVID-19 pandemic has revealed the persistent inequality in the gender distribution of unpaid care work with all of them indicating the unusual burden of domestic responsibilities with no assistance from men in doing household chores. ILO observes that prior to the COVID-19 crisis, over two third of 16.4 billion hours were spent by women in unpaid care work every day across the world. This has now increased manifold (ILO Brief, 2020a). This is more so in the case of poor domestic workers whose low pay and temporary employment has always undermined their capacity to hire paid labour to do care work in their families, thus adding to their paid care work responsibilities. During the lockdown and due to the pandemic, this unpaid care work in their own houses has intensified for the paid domestic workers. The absence of day care centres, schools and permanent presence of unemployed men demanding care along with the elderly care and increasing attention to sanitation have added to the woes of domestic workers doing unpaid family work. In addition, there are everyday ordeals of erratic water supply, lack of transport, lack of time to access ration shops, public hospitals, and corporation dispensaries faced by these workers.

Altogether, COVID-19 has exacerbated the crisis of existence for women domestic workers with their lack of access to labour and social protection including health care and maternity protection, especially when many of them with their reduced immunity are forced to work even under such life threatening conditions. Therefore, these women workers are, as ILO observes, likely to be more impoverished and marginalised from income replacement and from social protection schemes than the formal workers. It is also worth taking note of ILO's warning on lockdown measures here. It has said, '[l]ockdown measures will worsen poverty and vulnerabilities among the world's two billion informal economy workers' (ILO, 2020b).

Need for a coordinated social and health policy for domestic workers

More than ever before, in the present context of the pandemic it becomes important to recognise the domestic workers' economic productivity and their right to a safe healthy working environment. The state must take

effective measures in this direction. Incidentally, India has not even rati-
fied the ILO Convention on Domestic Workers which mandates nations to
provide occupational safety and health of these workers (ILO Domestic
Workers Convention, 2011).

Given the vulnerability of paid domestic workers, prioritising monetary
and health support along with meeting their immediate needs becomes a
state responsibility. In particular, the state has to attend to their special needs
of sanitation and health care and evolve specific social protection schemes.
About ten Central Trade Unions in India have already demanded immediate
measures from the state to protect the livelihood of vulnerable workers in
the informal sector including the migrant workers and for the inclusion of
trade unions in the COVID-19 response task force. The Central government
so far has not responded to these demands (ILO, 2020b).

Rethinking the role of Tamil Nadu Domestic Workers' Welfare Board

In consonance with the demands of the trade unions, the Tamil Nadu
Domestic Welfare Board may initiate few consultative processes with trade
unions that work for the welfare of domestic workers and include them as
part of the task force to address the specific needs of the domestic workers. In this regard, the Board must recognise specific gendered nature of
discriminations and exclusions that are faced by these workers during the
pandemic in order to prioritise their occupational health and livelihood
issues (ILO Brief, 2020b). In this regard ILO guideline on this might help
the state to evolve a coordinated health and social policy: '[s]trengthening
occupational safety and health, adjusting work arrangements, preventing
discrimination and exclusion, and providing access to health care and paid
leave (and also to food and social services for the most vulnerable) are all
indispensable strands of a coordinated health and social policy response
to the crisis' (ILO Policy Brief on Covid-19, Pillar:3). Treating domestic
workers as essential service workers and providing them with necessary
personal protective equipment along with reliable and accessible information and affordable health services is the responsibility of the Tamil Nadu
Domestic Workers' Welfare Board, who can be helped by the domestic
workers' unions. Simple measures like having mobile COVID-19 testing
centres placed in various public places where the workers could easily get
tested will help them and the state to contain the spread of virus. Similar
such demands have been placed by the International Domestic Workers'
Federation (IDWF, 18 March 2020).

Established in 2007, the Tamil Nadu Domestic Workers' Welfare Board
offers a range of financial assistance to the registered domestic workers ranging

from children's education, marriage, and maternal health expenses of the workers, death-related benefits for the worker's heir, a nominal pension amount, and so on. Unfortunately, the Welfare Board has not even paid attention to the compulsory registration of all domestic workers to benefit from these schemes. Domestic workers are not even aware of the existence of the Board. For this, the Board must adequately publicise their activities and schemes and evolve new norms and rules for compulsory registration of the workers.

In fixing the minimum wages for the domestic workers, the state has overlooked the problem of fixing the categories of domestic work as unskilled labour – cooking and childcare for instance – leading to low pay for these essential care workers. All these have serious implications for the dignity and decency of work for the domestic workers.

Being in informal work, no domestic worker has any legal entitlement to sickness leave benefits. In the present context of COVID-19, as ILO has pointed out, there is a need for a coordinated health and social welfare response to the crisis so that the state can ensure occupational safety, better working environment for these workers without discrimination and exclusion (ILO Policy Brief on Covid 19, Pillar: 3). To address specific health needs of the workers in times of pandemic like this, employers should be made to pay a nominal amount towards insurance scheme or other benefits for the workers.

Work from home (WFH) policy, mainly for the private-sector employees, may affect the paid domestic workers who work in such houses, as some workers anticipate increasing workloads with houses multiplying as office space with no additional wage for doing any extra cleaning or sanitation work. Some workers even expressed their anxiety about working for houses with bachelors who would be working from home.[7] Extending the laws related to sexual harassment at work to the domestic work sphere and improving wages for the increasing workload would enable these workers to feel safe at work. As we noted elsewhere, two legislations concerning domestic workers, The Unorganised Workers' Social Security Act, 2008 and The Sexual Harassment of Women at Workplace (Prevention, Prohibition and Redressal) Act, 2013, at present are inadequate in addressing the specific forms of exploitations peculiar to this work (Rajkotwala and Mehta, 2020).

With the postponement of school education, the likelihood of inducing young girls into paid domestic work will result in an increase in child labour in small towns and in rural Tamil Nadu (Kundu, 21 April 2020). Providing accessible technology-based educational solutions for vulnerable families could become an important solution to mitigate the problem of child labour (ILO Brief 2020a & 2020b).

As long-term measures to mitigate the vulnerability of paid domestic workers,[8] following steps can be taken by the state through the Domestic Welfare Board:

1) Formalisation of the domestic work sector through mandatory registration of domestic workers with the corporation divisions/wards.
2) Employment of only registered domestic workers and punitive measures for employers violating such norms. As the trade unions perceive such registration to have a benefit to both employer and domestic worker, it is a workable option.
3) Registered workers should be entitled to (a) living wage (time-rated or job-specified wages) to be fixed by the labour department; (b) decent working conditions to be clearly laid out; (c) guidelines for treatment of domestic workers; (d) leave, annual bonus, transport, etc., as part of the contract; (e) right to associate and freedom to participate in union activities; (f) right to access good public health centres near their homes; (g) right to information related to their welfare provided by the government through the Domestic Workers' Welfare Board.
4) The state could additionally levy tax through corporation to cover the cost of social security and insurance. The money collected from worker, employer, and the additional levies could form part of the Domestic Workers Fund. The existing Domestic Workers' Welfare Board could be the nodal body for the welfare and oversight.
5) Mandatory savings could be introduced through means of some co-operative efforts which might enable the domestic workers to utilise, borrow, and lend to other women during this kind of crisis.
6) Housing security could be provided for women workers to avoid eviction threat by landlords, state, and lenders. This is especially important in the light of rural migrant workers selling their small-sized patta lands in the village to buy non-patta land in the city for their permanent dwelling with little housing security.
7) Displacement of workers within the city which has huge social, economic, and health cost for the workers should be stopped.

For carrying out some of these welfare measures, the state Domestic Workers' Welfare Board could collaborate with Penn Thozhilalargal Sangam, Centre for Women's Development and Research (CWDR, Chennai), and ILO, Decent Work Program, Delhi, to create a framework or guidelines in the light of the present crisis and to look into aspects of laws, and their implementation.

***

Acknowledgements: We thank Sujatha Mody, Renuka Bala, and Karen Coelho for their valuable inputs, comments, and suggestions. Usual caveats apply.

Notes

1 According to this central government act, 'workman' connotes 'any person other than a person whose employment is of a casual nature and who is employed otherwise than for the purposes of the employer's trade or business'. The Act's definition of an employer and the contract labour though clearly applies to the paid domestic workers and their employers, the provisions of the Act have not been extended to cover the paid domestic work. See, 'The Workmen's Compensation Act, 1923', https://indiankanoon.org/doc/1806623/. (accessed on 20 October 2020).
2 Applying this Act to paid domestic work would have helped regulate this contractual work since one of the regulatory requirements under this statute include registration of the principle employer and the issue of licence to recruitment agencies as contractors. As of now these provisions exist only for work that involves establishments in which 20 or more workers are employed as contract labour and that they do not apply to 'establishments in which work only of an intermittent or casual nature is performed'.
3 In 2018, the Tamil Nadu government has fixed their minimum wage at Rs. 37 per hour and the monthly minimum wage at Rs.6,836 for 8 hours of work per day.
4 We have carried out few tele-interviews with a small number of domestic workers from north, south, and central Chennai and also received notes on challenges faced by the domestic workers during COVID-19 from domestic workers' forums led by Pen Thozhilalar Sangam (north Chennai) and Manushi, Centre for Women's Development Research (Greater Chennai Corporation).
5 In an informal chat, Sujatha Mody, an activist scholar with Pen Thozhilalar Sangam, claimed that more than 80 per cent of the women domestic workers of Chennai were not paid salary for at least two months during the lockdown.
6 Those with a ration card have received an allowance of Rs.1,000 along with substandard rice and lentils. This is not adequate for even a small family.
7 A domestic worker who works for the bachelor IT workers said that previously she used to enter their house only after they have left for work and therefore felt comfortable working for them. She expressed her fear that they might make it inconvenient for her to work when they are present in the house all the time and without any woman employer around in the house.
8 The ILO labour standards on employment, social protection, wage protection, and workplace cooperation already contain specific guidance on policy measures for various sets of workers such as paid domestic workers affected by COVID-19 related crisis. While drawing up our specific suggestions we have kept this in mind. See, 'ILO Standards and COVID-19 (coronavirus): Key provisions of international labour standards relevant to the evolving COVID-19 outbreak', https://www.ilo.org/wcmsp5/groups/public/---ed_norm/---normes/documents/genericdocument/wcms_739937.pdf. (accessed on 15 June 2020).

References

Coelho, Karen, T. Venkat and R. Chandrika. 2013. 'Housing, homes and domestic work: A study of paid domestic workers from resettlement colony in Chennai', *Economic and Political Weekly*, Vol. 48, No. 43.

DT Next. 2020. 'Residential colonies debate on allowing domestic helps to enter', June 10. https://www.dtnext.in/News/City/2020/05/04065718/1228201/Resident ial-colonies-debate-on-allowing-domestic-helps-.vpf (accessed on 15/6/2020).

IDWF. 2020. 'International domestic worker's federation statement on protecting domestic workers rights and fighting the Corona Virus pandemic', Mar 18. https ://idwfed.org/en/updates/global-idwf-statement-on-protecting-domestic-worke rs-rights-and-fighting-the-coronavirus-pandemic (accessed on 7/6/2020).

ILO. 2020a. 'ILO standards and COVID-19 (coronavirus): Key provisions of international labour standards relevant to the evolving COVID-19 outbreak', May 29. https://www.ilo.org/global/standards/WCMS_739937/lang--en/index.h tm (accessed on 15 June 2020).

ILO. 2020b. 'COVID-19 and the world of work: Country policy responses', October 9. https://www.ilo.org/global/topics/coronavirus/country-responses/lang--en/in dex.htm#IN (accessed on 20/10/2020).

ILO. n.d. 'Policy brief on COVID-19: Pillar 3: Protecting workers in the workplace', https://www.ilo.org/global/topics/coronavirus/impacts-and-responses/WCMS _739049/lang--en/index.htm (accessed on 16/6/2020).

ILO Brief. 2020a. 'COVID-19 crisis and the informal economy: Immediate responses and policy challenges', May 5. https://www.ilo.org/global/topics/e mployment-promotion/informal-economy/publications/WCMS_743623/lang- -en/index.htm (accessed on 14/6/2020).

ILO Brief. 2020b. 'The COVID-19 response: Getting gender equality right for a better future of women at work', May 11. https://www.ilo.org/global/topics/c oronavirus/WCMS_744685/lang--en/index.htm (accessed on 15/6/2020).

ILO Domestic Workers Convention. 2011. No. 189, Article 13. https://www.ilo.org/ dyn/normlex/en/f?p=NORMLEXPUB:12100:0::NO::P12100_INSTRUMENT _ID:2551460 (accessed on 13/6/2020).

ILO News. 2020. 'Contagion or starvation, the dilemma facing informal workers during the COVID-19 pandemic', May 7. https://www.ilo.org/global/about-th e-ilo/newsroom/news/WCMS_744005/lang--en/index.htm (accessed on 15/6/ 2020).

Kundu, Protiva. 2020. 'COVID-19 crisis will push millions of children into child labour', *Wire*, April 21. https://thewire.in/rights/covid-19-crisis-will-push-mil lions-of-vulnerable-children-into-child-labour (accessed on 13/6/2020).

Rajkotwala, Mustafa and Rahil Mehta. 2020. 'Lockdown woes : The dismal state of domestic workers in India', *Jurist*, May 6. https://www.jurist.org/commentary/t ag/author-mustafa-rajkotwala-and-rahil-mehta/ (accessed on 16 /6/2020).

Ramakrishnan, Susmitha. 2020. 'With no pay, hopes dry up for domestic helps in Chennai', *The New Indian Express*, June 12. https://www.newindianexpress.c om/cities/chennai/2020/may/18/with-no-pay-hopes-dry-up-for-domestic-helps-i n-chennai-2144681.html (accessed on 16/6/2020).

Sarkar, Kingshuk. 2019. 'Complexity in the determination of minimum wages for the domestic workers in India', *NLI Research Studies Series*, 137/2019. https ://vvgnli.gov.in/sites/default/files/137-2019-Kingshuk_Sarkar.pdf (accessed on 14/6/2020).

Tamil Nadu Government. 2020. *Revenue and Disaster Management (DMII) Department, G.O (D) No. 195.* March 30. https://tnsdma.tn.gov.in/app/webroot/img/covid_19/gos/lockdown/G.O.195.pdf (accessed on 20/10/2020).

The Hindu. 2020. 'Domestic workers in Chennai face stigma, many are left without jobs', September 3. https://www.thehindu.com/news/national/tamil-nadu/domestic-workers-in-chennai-face-stigma-many-are-left-without-jobs/article32513338.ece (accessed on 15 /9/2020).

The Newsminute. 2020. 'Facing job loss and stigma, hundreds of domestic workers protest in Chennai', September 02. https://www.thenewsminute.com/article/facing-job-loss-and-stigma-hundreds-domestic-workers-protest-chennai-132111 (accessed on 15/9/2020).

Viswanath, Kalpana. 2020. 'It is time to stop seeing domestic workers as COVID-19 carriers', *The Wire*, May 27. https://thewire.in/labour/covid-19-lockdown-domestic-workers (accessed on 15/6/2020).

9 Controlling journeys, controlling labour

COVID-19 and migrants

Pushpendra and Manish K Jha

Introduction

The complete lockdown announced by the prime minister of India on 24 March 2020 was followed by episodes of hundreds of thousands of migrants defying the lockdown and walking towards their home, sometimes covering more than a thousand kilometres. These journeys not only exposed the vulnerabilities of migrant labourers but also brought the issue of their return into political discourse. However, the majority of workers, particularly long-distance ones, remained stranded for want of public transport. The media extensively reported their ordeal at the destination and their protests in different parts of the country demanding return journey. Questions were asked as to why the Government of India did not anticipate the mass exodus of inter-state and intra-state migrants before announcing the lockdown. Why did the government not give a one-week window for the migrants to return to their homes by public transport, particularly trains, when the case-load of coronavirus was minuscule?[1] Why did the government take the risk of alienating this vast number of the workforce of the country despite India being an electoral democracy?

The chapter attempts to engage with these questions by using the concept of labour-control regime. The analyses of various events and incidents during the pandemic illustrate how the regime of labour control is embedded in the state's strategy of dealing with the pandemic which shaped the state's policy towards journeys of migrants. We discuss how the state's strategy of labour control has created a crisis of legitimacy for the state and given rise to new conflicts that define the emerging state-labour relations. We also look at various measures by the state aimed at exerting control over labour which will have far-reaching consequences for state-labour relations.

Labour-control regime: How the state and capital strategise?

The labour-control regime refers to the social need in capitalism for integrating labour into the production system and labour processes by a variety of means, directly and coercively, as well as indirectly and reciprocally (Jonas 2009). Various factors facilitate workers' integration – knowing the employer, social networks around the place/region, developing skill in the work, specific practices such as employer allowing the workers to use the workplace as accommodation, caste- and region-based recruitment, and the presence of a labour contractor.

Labour control is easier particularly when the labour market has migrants and casual workers, production takes place outside of the organised sector, where trade unions are weak or absent, and labour market allows flexibility in terms of sub-contracting and flexible work schedules. Labour control also demands that state regulations be weak, allowing unregulated terms and conditions of employment, unwritten contract, with weak oversight and redressal system for abuses of labour rights. The fragmentation of production processes at multiple layers through work process sub-contracting has made labour relations complicated in which employers turn out to be distant and invisible. Violation of workers' rights is easier in the absence of a clear lineage of accountability. The control regime is premised on the understanding that the protection regime, its nemesis, is antithetical to ease of business, which in turn is construed as a *sine qua non* for attracting big-ticket investments, particularly foreign direct investments. In a capitalist economy, the state works on behalf of capital to ensure a conducive institutional environment. It uses regulation as a function of control, a crucial tool for establishing a regime of labour control.

The labour control is exercised through the institutional measures aimed at incorporating labour either through restriction or through co-option (Fishwick 2018). Institutional co-option measures are less explicitly authoritarian and intended to domesticate labour (O'Donnell 1988). Capital and regime friendly trade unions, the network of labour contractors, and co-opting labour relations through caste, kinship, region, religion, and other identity markers contribute to creating disciplined and docile labour in non-conflictual ways. Other ways of co-option are re-organisation of the workplace to make it informal, employer's paternalistic relations with the labour and social welfare measures by the state. However, for the state, the most crucial role lies in creating a restrictive institutional environment through various institutional measures involving various arms of the state – legislative, juridical, and executive. The most common measures are legal restrictions on organising, mobilising, and representing workers, dilution of wages and collective bargaining rights, removal of legal protections, and autonomy to the employer in exercising labour control practices (Fishwick 2018). State violence is integral to it as the state often resorts to using brute force to create a general sense of fear for seeking compliance, and whenever there are protests and resistance against its agenda.

In the following pages, drawing from published empirical accounts in newspapers and news portals, we intend to discuss the configuration of control over migrants' return exercised by the state and employers through state and private institutions during the pandemic.

The first wave of workers' return migration

Let us return to the question – did the government not anticipate the exodus of migrant workers when it announced a very stringent lockdown from the midnight of 24 March? The sequence of events, reported in newspapers, television channels, and news portals strongly suggests otherwise. Below we try to reconstruct the chronology of some important events to make our point.

With the declaration of COVID-19 a national disaster on 14 March, most of the state governments instructed shutting of multiplexes, cinema halls, educational institutions till 31 March. By this time, jobs had started dwindling as factories, shops and establishments, transport, construction, and service sector were either closing or reducing the scale of their activities. Workers were staring at an uncertain future. They feared for their lives as they continued to live and work in too crowded conditions and, hence, unable to follow instructions like 'social distancing.'

The exodus of migrant labour from megacities had started quite early. Newspapers reported large crowds at the Mumbai, Pune, Delhi, and other railway stations. Many of them had the stamp of 'quarantine' on their hands. On 21 March, the *Indian Express* reported how in the aftermath of Maharashtra government's order to shut down shops and establishments until 31 March, the exodus began in Mumbai and Pune with tens of thousands of workers lining up at ticket counters and gathering on platforms as they waited for trains to take them home, mostly in Uttar Pradesh and Bihar.[2]

A similar multi-city report on 21 March 2020 carried out by the news portal, Scroll.in reported widespread return of migrants from various cities as the migrant workers faced the prospect of increasing loss of livelihoods, hunger, fast depleting savings, and uncertain futures.[3] On the next day, 22 March, a news item in the *Indian Express* reported similar situation from cities like Chennai, Guwahati, Hyderabad, Kochi, Mumbai, Pune, and

Delhi. Migrants feared that the Railways could potentially switch off their services.[4]

Unaware of the Centre's plans, the Central Railway announced to run special trains, mostly with sleeper and unreserved coaches, to the eastern and northern parts of the country to deal with the rush for the return journey by migrants. However, to mark the Prime Minister's call for Janata Curfew, the Railways cancelled all 3,700 trains across the country scheduled for departure between 21 March, midnight, and 10 pm on 22 March.

That the political establishment knew the exodus had already begun is corroborated by the fact that ahead of the Janata Curfew on 22 March, Prime Minister Narendra Modi appealed to the migrants on 20 March, 'I appeal to my brothers and sisters who are moving to their villages over the fear of the coronavirus to stay where you are for the next few days. Travelling in the crowd increases the risk of the virus spreading. It puts at risk the people from your villages, and will add to the difficulties of your families'.[5] It would have been anybody's guess that migrants would attempt to get home if they lost their job or means of livelihood. Clearly, despite the evolving migrant crisis, the prime minister decided to go ahead with announcing the nationwide lockdown, perhaps the strictest in the world. By assuring people of winning the war against the epidemic in 21 days, the government was projecting COVID-19 as a short-term disaster, so that migrant workers need not leave their workplace. We contend that the sequence of events from pre-lockdown to post-lockdown till date, as we will discuss later, clearly establish the state's efforts to control the labour but without any accountability of their well-being. More than the spread of the virus, a future spectre of labour shortage was haunting the capital and the government.

Our argument is based on four observations: first, the electoral promises of the Modi government to overhaul 'restrictive' labour laws in India to align with its slogan of 'Make in India' and 'Ease of Business'. The government had proposed drastic changes in the existing labour laws and amalgamating 44 central labour laws into four labour codes. The Parliament had already passed the Code on Wages before the pandemic; the rest three were passed during the lockdown. The pandemic provided the right opportunity to push labour reforms with little possibility of opposition, particularly on the streets. Second, the government was on a privatisation spree of the existing public sector companies. Besides being an important economic agenda of the government, privatisation promised to be a vital source for generating revenues in the backdrop of the state's inability to raise revenues under the new Goods and Services Tax. Sweeping changes in industrial relations were deemed necessary to create a trouble-free private labour market and market-labour relations. Third, the sickeningly unsafe living conditions in workers habitats incompatible with 'social distancing', lack of substantive savings by migrants given their low earnings (Pushpendra and Singh 2020), and the hostile middle class (Jha and Deeksha 2021) cannot be addressed in short-run, that too during an epidemic. That migrants' well-being does not matter and they are disposable did reflect in the Garib Kalyan Yojana which did not provide direct cash support to migrants. Besides, the existing social security architecture does not offer any substantive support during disasters. There was little room for any co-option measure. Fourth, a general lack of clarity about the virus which led the establishment to believe it as a short-term epidemic. In the backdrop of an ailing economy, on a steep downward slope, the government and the private capital were anxious to ensure availability of labour immediately after the lockdown was relaxed and eventually lifted.

The strategy of control over labour through control over return journey of migrants gradually became apparent, particularly in the next phase, starting with the complete lockdown from 25 March. How the state and its institutions changed from largely passive observers to active enforcers of control regime will be discussed in the subsequent pages.

Exodus after lockdown: The second wave

While the migrants were gradually leaving the cities, the announcement of a 'curfew-like' lockdown proved to be the tipping point. Migrants defied the lockdown and started to flee the cities. The most haunting images that all of us confronted were of those lakhs of migrants who, in the absence of any public transport, trekked hundreds and, in innumerable cases, even more than a thousand of kilometres. Forced upon them, these were perilous journeys – by foot, on the bicycle, hiding in trucks or tankers, along railway tracks, or using a mix of all these and several others means, without or with little money and food. As the receiving states of Uttar Pradesh, Bihar, Jharkhand, Odisha, Rajasthan, Madhya Pradesh, Chhattisgarh, and West Bengal looked helpless and inadequately prepared to respond to the unfolding humanitarian crisis, the Centre asked state governments and union territories to seal borders to stop the movement of migrant workers effectively. Migrants encountered emergence of unanticipated new borders, officials with an obsession to contain the contagion through travelling body/spreader, accidents, and death. The instances of travelling workers beaten up, sprayed with disinfectant chemicals, and harassed and harangued by lockdown enforcing hostile administration on highways, city/town borders, and zones were abounding as they had supposedly disturbed the lockdown prescription, the disease containment plan, and other control mechanisms. The Centre had clearly asked for anyone on the roads to be treated as a violator of the lockdown, leaving them vulnerable to more mistreatment and violence from the state.[6]

Though Delhi and Uttar Pradesh governments initially took a lenient view on the transfer of inter-state workers from Delhi to Uttar Pradesh (and also Bihar), the Centre on 29 March instructed to effectively seal the district and state borders and not to allow any movement of people across cities or on highways.[7] Following this, the DGP of Haryana stated that those travelling by foot on highways and roads 'should be picked up, placed in buses and left in localities from where they started'. He went on to say that big indoor stadiums or other similar facilities be turned into 'temporary jails' so that people who refused to obey the lawful directions of district administration could be arrested and placed in custody for the offence committed by them under the Disaster Management Act.[8] Numerous control mechanisms were put in operation through a series of notifications.

On 29 March, the Ministry of Home Affairs (MHA), issued an order[9] that all the employers, be it in the industry or the shops and commercial establishments, shall make payment of wages of their workers, at their workplaces, on the due date, without any deduction, for the period their establishments are under closure during the lockdown. However, a rapid survey by Safe in India and Agrasar (n.d.) of 100 migrant workers, who had decided to stay back in Gurugram, revealed that around 75 per cent of the workers were not paid for April which was a 'massive worsening' over March 2020, for which around 25 per cent did not receive their full wages in clear violation of the government order.[10] Newspaper reports suggest that such violations were the rule rather than an exception. Later, on 4 June, the Supreme Court ordered not to take any coercive action against employers concerning the MHA order mentioned above. Legal validity apart, the order seemed to be designed to fail, at best as camouflage for the state's unwillingness to adopt any co-option measure for workers.

The state's intention to aggressively follow restrictive measures was evident not only in controlling the transport but also in its other measures. The prime minister had set up a COVID-19 Economic Response Task Force on 19 March to create an emergency package. The package, announced on 25 March, focused on domicile-based relief and had hardly anything for migrants stranded at the destination.[11] The government knew that most of the social security schemes did not have portability provisions. A good example is the fund available under the Building and Other Construction Workers Welfare Boards. The Centre directed the states to support construction workers from the fund. However, due to domicile-based registration and the absence of portability, migrants had little access to the funds. In Bihar, for example, the state government did not register any new construction worker under the fund after the Centre's directive. Only those migrant workers who had prior-registration in the state could get Rs. 2,000 transferred by the state board. However, in the absence of disaggregated data, there is no way to know the exact number of beneficiary migrants.[12]

The institution of judiciary supplemented the regime of labour control in several instances of omission and commission in its approach to the migrant issue. In response to a petition seeking relief for migrants attempting to return home during the 21-day lockdown, the Supreme Centre accepted the Centre's submission that there were no migrant workers on the roads 'as of 11 am on 31 March', and they had all been taken to the nearest available shelter. The Court did not even feel the need to verify facts independently. Moreover, the Court expressed satisfaction with the steps taken by the government and declined to intervene. The court even went to the extent of saying that the migrants' exodus was due to the panic created by fake news.[13]

While police everywhere turned ruthless in controlling the mobility of migrants, protests erupted at several places, sometimes turning violent. On 30 March, the situation took a violent turn in Surat when police tried to stop about 500 textile factory workers who were mostly migrants from Uttar Pradesh, Bihar, Madhya Pradesh, and Chhattisgarh. On 10 April, 80 migrant labourers were arrested in Lakshana area of Surat for defying the lockdown and going on a rampage. The workers were demanding that they be handed over their wages and allowed to return to Odisha, their home state. Most of these workers were employees of the power loom textile factories which had been shut and were not paying the workers their daily wages.[14]

Hoping that trains would resume on 14 April after the end of the 3-week lockdown, at least 3,000 migrant workers gathered at Bandra station in Mumbai, but the police dispersed them by using force.[15] On 27 April, a group of construction workers protested and pelted stones at the office of Dream City Diamond Bourse in Surat. Alleging that they were made to work amid coronavirus lockdown, workers demanded that they be sent back to their native places. The state government had permitted construction to go ahead with conditions applied in order to meet the revised target date of completion of the project by March 2021.[16]

Even in rural areas, migrants were put under confinement and forced to work. A case in Bardoli in South Gujarat was reported of sugarcane harvesters who were not allowed to return to their villages after completing their work for one sugar factory by another factory which was facing a shortage of labour. In order to avoid disruption in production, the district administration allowed sugar factories to send lorries to various villages across the Dang district to transport workers back to the fields, but the same administration would not let workers go back home.[17]

As the above narratives suggest, the fact that the state went in full force to restrict the mobility of migrants even without a contingency plan to address their immediate vulnerabilities, demonstrates how migrants have no power to put constraints on the state policy. Instead, they are subject to the exercise of state power, in its most callous and violent forms. It also exposed the fragmentation of labour and their organisation. Did the state lose legitimacy before labour? What did the state achieve through restrictive policy when ultimately it had to loosen restrictions on mobility? There are analytical limitations on answers to these questions, as the impact of state action will take a longer time to unfold.

The third wave of the return journey: New tricks of control

The Centre announced Shramik special trains from 1 May on May Day. However, the journey was highly controlled, and the system was procedurally complicated, migrant unfriendly, and created confusion. The unprepared, hence reluctant, receiving states gave consent for a limited number of trains. Then arose the issue of who will pay the train fare. Initially the fare, with a corona surcharge of Rs. 50, was collected from the workers. Later, state governments agreed to pay the fare. The Railways, which could run more than 12,000 trains every day before the pandemic, ran just a few hundred for months. On top of it, the routes of some trains were diverted delaying their journeys by several additional days. Moreover, inadequate food and water arrangements added to the woes of the passengers. Ninety-six passengers reportedly died during the train journeys.[18]

This approach of the government was in sharp contrast to the usual approach of the state regarding workers journey. The state has been interventionist in expediting the journey of workers by facilitating journeys of migrants from labour surplus areas to labour deficient areas or areas/sectors/industries that prefer migrant labour. When the Green Revolution was introduced in the mid-sixties in selected regions of the country, it introduced new trains to specifically ensure functional connectivity between source and destination geographies (Das 1992). An elaborate but systematic rail and road network operated to ensure the smooth supply of cheap labour for meeting the demands of several sectors in the cities and also rural areas. At the same time, the state has remained *non-interventionist* in various dimensions of labour life worlds such as rental housing market, wages, labour welfare, and their working and living conditions which remain firmly in the grip of the market mechanism. Both measures of intervention and non-intervention are selective. The state's facilitating role of labour's journey in the pre-corona times, and its muted response to the issue of their return journey during corona times, served the same purpose – controlling the labour flow for the industry.

The influence of builders' lobby that prompted the Karnataka government to cancel the special train for the stranded migrants is another example of how the anxiety of the capital prevailed over migrants' right to return home. Following a meeting between the Confederation of Real Estate Developers' Association of India (CREDAI), Karnataka and Chief Minister B.S. Yeddyurappa, the state government wrote to the Railways cancelling all inter-state trains from Karnataka. The CM told that the state was looking to restart its construction sector, for which migrant labourers were the backbone. An exodus would have affected the sector. Bengaluru MP Tejasvi Surya hailed the decision as a 'bold' move to help migrants 'restart their dreams' in the city. Subsequently, labour agitations and even some confrontation with the police were reported across the city. It is to be noted that between 3 May and 5 May, the state government received online registration on its portal from over 2.13 lakh migrant workers for their return journey by train. The state government finally relented and formally requested the Railways for at least 14 trains between 8 May and 15 May to key sending states.[19]

Legislative route to labour control during the pandemic

Controlling the journey was also accompanied by making changes in labour laws through ordinance routes. At least ten states, including Haryana, Himachal Pradesh, Gujarat, Rajasthan, Madhya Pradesh, Odisha, Assam, Maharashtra, Goa, Punjab, and Uttarakhand, have changed their labour laws by amending provisions or suspending some others. The changes allow industries in Rajasthan, Gujarat, Himachal Pradesh, and Uttar Pradesh to force labourers to work 72 hours a week, an increase of 24 hours from the earlier stipulated 48 hours. In effect, a labourer could be forced to work up to 12 hours a day on 6 working days of a week, from an earlier schedule of eight hours a day. That went against the International Labour Organisation (ILO) Convention on hours of work to which India is a signatory.[20] In Gujarat and Uttar Pradesh, the industries were not even required to pay 'overtime' to labourers working in the factories. Except for Haryana, all other states announced this change to be in force for three months. Gujarat announced that except for laws pertaining to the payment of minimum wages, safety norms and compensation for workers in case of industrial accidents, no other provisions of the labour law would apply to all new companies that wished to operate in the state for at least 1,200 days, and for those that had already been operational for that period. The state government also offered land and infrastructure for companies and projects that were looking to shift base from China.[21] These measures shed light on the approach of state governments on state-labour relations which are headed towards extreme exploitation of labour.

However, more extensive labour reforms, with far-reaching consequences, came in the form of three new labour codes passed on 23 September by the Parliament – Industrial Relations Code, Code on Social Security, and Occupational Safety, Health and Working Conditions Code. The scope of the chapter does not allow us to discuss the merits of these codes in detail. However, it is worth noting that all labour unions of the country have vehemently opposed them for imposing legal restrictions on organising and representing workers and their collective bargaining rights, for removing several legal protections and bestowing enormous power to employers to exercise labour-control practices. On the crucial Industrial Relations Code, Sundar (2020) suggests that it will fail to create a conducive and efficient industrial relations environment, and will neither promote the ease of doing business nor serve workers' welfare. These three codes, together with the Code on Wages, have not only dashed any hope for workers rights and decent work condition but also given a massive push towards further flexibilisation of work and employment.

Conclusion

This chapter engages with the idea and strategies of controlling the flow of migrants' return journey which has so far been a neglected subject. As Samaddar (2020: 44) points out, 'In the annals of migration the issue of return was never given importance to the degree attention was paid to the issue of entry and work, whether in refugee and migration literature or in the discussion on racism and xenophobia that makes migrants the victim within a country'. Controlling the onward journey of internal migrants is likely to be an act of son-of-the-soil politics or xenophobia or competition between local and outside workers – more associated with the social and political domain. However, the capital and, for its sake, the state seek to ensure the flow of incoming workers. The return journey must follow a predictable pattern which is often based on trade-offs between the interests of the capital and labour, with the balance heavily tilted towards the former. Any exodus threatens to disrupt the predictable pattern triggering the need for control measures.

The pandemic and resultant exodus presented a real possibility of disrupting the pattern. The government could effectively control the return journey, which exposed the fragmentation of labour and their vastly diminished power to exercise constraints on the state policy. The proliferation of work outside the organised sector has created the ground for this situation. The state could get away with virtually disowning the responsibility of feeding, safety, and security of migrants in cities, making them further pauperised and traumatised. Legislative and legal institutions have further strengthened the labour-control regime. The state has been successful in creating a new labour-state relation that marks an end to the rhetoric of labour welfarism.

However, the state's attempts to control migrants' return journeys and also fundamentally change the state-labour relations through newer control mechanisms have met with resistance and struggles of migrants. Their silent defiance of the lockdown has also exposed limitations of the state's capacity to enforce complete control over workers' decision-making and their body. As the impact of the labour-control regime will gradually unfold its impact in the times ahead, we may witness a renewed and sustained struggle between the state and market forces on the one side and migrants and other workers on the other.

Notes

1 On 24 March, the total number of infected persons in the country was only 564 and the chances of spread of the virus by the journey of migrant workers were negligible.
2 Siddique, Iram, Ajay Jadhav. 2020. "Covid-19: Exodus from Mumbai, Pune as migrant workers pack trains headed East." *The Indian Express*, March 21. Retrieved from https://indianexpress.com/article/coronavirus/coronavirus-india-mumbai-pune-migrant-workers-6324722/. *The Indian Express*. Accessed on 10 October 2020.
3 Daniyal, Shoaib, Supriya Sharma and Naresh Fernandes. 2020. "As Covid-19 pandemic hits India's daily-wage earners hard, some leave city for their home towns." *The Indian Express*, March 21. Retrieved from https://scroll.in/article/956779/starvation-will-kill-us-before-corona-the-covid-19-pandemic-has-hit-indias-working-class-hard. Accessed on 10 October 2020.
4 Varma, Vishnu, Rahul V Pisharody, Janardhan Koushik, Tora Agarwala. 2020. "COVID-19: As migrant workers return home, how different states are feeling the pinch." *The Indian Express*, March 22. Retrieved from https://indianexpress.com/article/india/coronavirus-migrant-workers-kerala-bengal-tamil-nadu-6326896/. Accessed on 10 October 2020.
5 Express Web Desk. 2020. "'Stay wherever you are to stop coronavirus': PM's fresh appeal ahead of 'Janata curfew'." *The Indian Express*. March 21. Retrieved from https://indianexpress.com/article/coronavirus/coronavirus-pm-modi-appeals-people-to-stay-where-you-are-ahead-of-janata-curfew-6325761/. Accessed on 10 October 2020.
6 Express Web Desk. 2020. "Exodus of migrants, death on roads, relief package: Week 1 highlights of India lockdown." *The Indian Express*, April 1. Retrieved from https://indianexpress.com/article/coronavirus/coronavirus-india-lockdown-week-1-highlights-migrants-6342355/. Accessed on 24 October 2020.
7 The Wire Staff. 2020. "'Seal All Borders': Centre Decides to Stop Long Walk Home of Migrant Labourers." *The Wire*, March 29. Retrieved from https://thewire.in/government/centre-migrant-labourers-walk-lockdown. Accessed on 24 October 2020.
8 The Wire Staff. 2020. "With Temporary Shelters, Haryana and UP Try to Stop Migrant Labourers From Walking to Villages." *The Wire*, March 30. Retrieved from https://thewire.in/rights/with-temporary-shelters-haryana-and-up-try-to-stop-migrant-labourers-from-walking-to-villages. Accessed on 24 October 2020.

9 Ministry of Home Affairs, Government of India, Order No. 40-3/2020-DM-I(A) dated 29 March 2020.
10 Safe in India and Agrasar. N.D. "Unworthy (Who will pay the April Salaries of Migrant Workers Now?)". Retrieved from https://60d15e1f-27ff-4be1-8827-f7f0b5f74084.filesusr.com/ugd/5d022b_97c80265b3994b6e95792dc304b4f4a8.pdf. Accessed on 25 October 2020.
11 Before the Pradhan Mantri Garib Kalyan Yojana was announced, the Working People's Charter, a network of organisations working with informal sector workers, on 22 March urged the Centre to create an emergency fund of Rs. 50,000 crore to provide social and economic support to workers in the informal sector. The demand included, among others, food package for at least three months and an 'immediate cash transfer' of Rs. 10,000 for one month to all types of workers and agricultural farmers. It also urged the Centre to impose a ban in reduction of workforce in small and medium enterprises, arrangements to freeze any kind of eviction notices for homes and mortgage payments, and suspending utility bills for a period of at least two months. For details see, https://workingpeoplescharter.in/main-pages/pandemic-and-impact/. Accessed on 12 October 2020.
12 Based on authors' query with a senior officer of the Department of Labour Resources, Government of Bihar (name is not disclosed for the sake of confidentiality).
13 Scroll Staff. 2020. "Coronavirus: 'No migrant workers on roads as of 11 am,' Centre tells Supreme Court." *Scroll.in*, March 31. Retrieved from https://scroll.in/latest/957784/coronavirus-no-migrant-workers-on-roads-as-of-11-am-centre-tells-supreme-court. Accessed on 22 October 2020.
14 The Wire Staff. 2020. "Surat: Migrant Workers Defy Lockdown, Demand Wages and Return to Home State." *The Wire*, April 11. Retrieved from https://thewire.in/rights/surat-migrant-workers-covid-19-lockdown-wages. Accessed on 24 October 2020.
15 Shantha, Sukanya. 2020. "'Let us Go Home': No Sign of Relief in PM's Speech, Migrant Workers Take to Mumbai Streets." *The Wire*, April 14. Retrieved from https://thewire.in/labour/mumbai-bandra-migrant-covid-19. Accessed on 24 October 2020.
16 "Laborers again protest at Surat Dream City Diamond Bourse construction site." *Desh Gujarat*, April 28, 2020. Retrieved from https://www.deshgujarat.com/2020/04/28/laborers-again-protest-at-sura-dream-city-diamond-bourse-construction-site/. Accessed on 6 October 2020.
17 Rose, Anushka. 2020. "Gujarat: Migrant Sugarcane Harvesters Are Forced to Work Through the Pandemic." *The Wire*, April 16. Retrieved from https://thewire.in/labour/gujarat-migrant-sugarcane-harvesters-covid-19. Accessed on 19 October 2020.
18 GN, Thejesh. N.D. "No virus deaths." *Blogsite of Thejesh GN*, Retrieved from https://thejeshgn.com/projects/covid19-india/non-virus-deaths/. Accessed on 19 October 2020.
19 Arakal, Ralph Alex. 2020. "To 'revive economy', Karnataka govt cancels special trains for migrants." *The Indian Express*, May 6. Retrieved from https://indianexpress.com/article/india/karnataka-govt-cancels-special-trains-for-migrants-to-revive-economy-6396185/. Accessed on 6 October 2020.
20 International Labour Organisation. N.D. "Forced Labour Convention, 1930 (No. 29)." Retrieved from https://www.ilo.org/dyn/normlex/en/f?p=NORMLEXPUB:12100:0::NO::P12100_ILO_CODE:C029. Accessed on 18 October 2020.

21 Umarji, Vinay. 2020. "After UP, Gujarat Offers 1,200-Day Labour Law Exemptions for New Industrial Investments." *The Wire*, May 9. Retrieved from https://thewire.in/economy/gujarat-labour-law-exemption-new-industries-covid-19. Accessed on 18 October 2020.

References

Das, Arvind N. 1992. *The Republic of Bihar*. New Delhi: Penguin Books.

Fishwick, Adam. 2018. Labour Control and Developmental State Theory: A New Perspective on Import-substitution Industrialization in Latin America. *Development and Change* 50(3): 655–678.

Jha, Manish K and Deeksha. 2021 (forthcoming). The Middle Class and the Migrant: Contention in The City. In Manish K Jha and Pushpendra (eds.). *Beyond Consumption: India's New Middle Class in the Neo-Liberal Times*. New Delhi: Routledge.

Jonas, A.E.G. 2009. Labour Control Regime. In N. J. Thrift and Rob Kitchin (eds.). *International Encyclopaedia of Human Geography*. Amsterdam, London, Oxford: Elsevier, 59–65.

O'Donnell, G. 1988. Bureaucratic Authoritarianism: Argentina, *1966–1973, in Comparative Perspective*. Berkeley, CA: University of California Press.

Pushpendra and Dipak Kumar Singh. 2020. Mobility and Threshold Social Security. In Nripendra Kishore Mishra (ed.). *Development Challenges of India After Twenty Five Years of Economic Reforms: Inequality, Labour, Employment and Migration*. Singapore: Springer.

Samaddar, Ranabir. 2020. Burdens *of an Epidemic: A Policy Perspective on COVID-19 and Migrant Labour*. Kolkata: Calcutta Research Group.

Sundar, K.R.Shyam. 2020. Critiquing the Industrial Relations Code Bill, 2019. *Economic and Political Weekly* 55(32–33): 45–48.

Index

Note: *Italic* page numbers refer to figures and page number followed by 'n' refer to endnote.

For Product Safety Concerns and Information please contact our EU
representative GPSR@taylorandfrancis.com
Taylor & Francis Verlag GmbH, Kaufingerstraße 24, 80331 München, Germany